A FEW CARDS
SHORT

A FEW CARDS SHORT

CALEN TEMPLETON

Calen Templeton

These are my memories, from my perspective,
and I have tried to represent events as faithfully as possible.
I have changed some names to protect
individuals' privacy.

To request permissions, contact the publisher at Crazycal179@sbc-
global.net

Paperback: 9781087976150
Ebook: 9781087976181

Cover Art: Kenny Peris
Layout/Cover Design/Editor: Emily Templeton

For Mom

"I forgot to tell you I love you."

"You know, I don't think you've ever said that to me before."

"Yeah, but I meant it every day."

-Dragon: The Bruce Lee Story

Introduction

This book is not meant to be read all in one sitting. And not even all in order. There are fifty-two short stories that were not written in chronological order or connected in any way, other than being about my life and adventures.

These stories are accurate and truthful to the best of my recollection, but most of them are from many years ago. I have told each of them dozens of times with slight changes, elaborations, and exaggerations over the years.

To read these stories as planned, I recommend getting a deck of cards, shuffling them, and picking a card at random. Find the chapter that goes with that card and begin. Repeat once a week, over the course of a year, until you get through them all.

I used my friends' real names whenever I thought it was appropriate. Throughout my life, I knew a few kids who shared the same name. I changed a few of them to avoid confusion.

If you knew me as a kid and recognize yourself in one of these stories and are offended, please know that I didn't intend to make you look bad. Or worse than me, at least.

Feel free to contact me and I will make amends. You can cash in three free Butts Up! shots. (A♣)

-Calen Templeton

Ace of Hearts

My best friend the summer after Freshman year was Eric. He is not important to this story after this paragraph, but him failing some of his classes is what started a chain reaction leading to the most awkward date I have ever been on. Now pay close attention. Eric and I were going to be in the tenth grade, but he had summer school. Summer school was in the next city over and all grades went to the same place for these classes. He met a girl who was a year younger than us, but she had failed or was held back twice. This put her in seventh grade. (I honestly don't remember her name and wouldn't use it here if I did. For the sake of avoiding an overabundance of female pronouns, I'll call her Brittany.) They started dating and I saw Brittany a few times. She was so excited for me to meet her best friend, thinking we would be a perfect couple, and I gave her my number to pass along.

Even before summer vacation ended, Eric and Brittany had broken up which should have been the end of this short story. But, the following week, my phone rang. It was her friend and she was delighted to meet me over the phone. We talked often and were getting along rather well. We tried to meet in person, but we lived pretty far from each other and she was grounded for her poor grades so she was limited to when she could go out.

When the school year started, we were still limited to a relationship over the phone but finally had a real-life date planned at an upcoming high school football game. The Friday night game was the only time she was allowed out of her house to meet me while she was still grounded. After about a month of talking with her once or twice a week, she was telling me about her day at school. Her classes were not very interesting but I listened politely as a possible soon-to-be boyfriend should. Then she mentioned something that I thought was rather peculiar. She said someone was giving her trouble at recess...

Wait, what!? Did she say recess? No, I must have misheard her.

I made up an excuse and hung up on her. I called Brittany. "How old is your friend? What grade is she in!?"

"She's a year behind me. I'm in sixth and she's in fifth grade." Remember Brittany was in sixth but was fourteen, the age of an eighth-grader and only two years younger than me and my friends.

"Holy hell! She's eleven! Why didn't you ever tell me that!?"

"I didn't think it mattered. Age is just a number, after all."

"Of course you don't know the difference. You failed and got held back twice!" I hung up on her and called my soon-to-be ex-girlfriend back. I don't know if that's right. We had never met in person and weren't officially dating yet. I guess we skipped that step and jumped ahead to the breakup. This might have been the shortest relationship in history.

"I'm really sorry, I can't go to that football game with you." I tried to let her down lightly, but she wasn't taking it well.

"What do you mean you can't go? I already bought the tickets!"

"I didn't know you were so young. It wouldn't be right."

"But Brittany said you love me! I've been talking about you at recess for a week. Everyone's going to think I'm a liar if you don't show up!"

"What did Brittany say!? I hardly even know you."

"You can't do this to me, I'll die!" She was crying now - bawling. I could only try to imagine what her tiny prepubescent tear-streaked face looked like since I'd never seen her before and didn't know what she looked like.

"I'm really sorry," I said again, quietly this time. It didn't mean anything and didn't hold any weight. "I have to go."

I felt really bad and she was crying harder now. I didn't know what else to say so I hung up the phone. My mom came into the kitchen, where our only phone in the house was, and sat down to talk to me.

"You have to go to that football game, you know." She said calmly.

"Mom, I can't. She's only eleven! What would people say?"

"It's not even your school, no one will know you there. It's only one night for you but this is going to crush that poor girl. She'll never get over it. Trust me, I know."

I knew my mom was right, she always was. Damnit! I called my date back and told her I'd meet her at the game as planned. We would meet outside since she had my ticket. But how would I know it was her? She had the idea to make a sign with my name like limo drivers do at the airport. She would hold it up at the entrance to point herself out to me.

My mom dropped me off at the high school stadium and I started looking around for my date among the crowd of people milling around the entrance waiting to enter. It didn't take long to find the girl jumping up and down excitedly waving a piece of notebook paper high above her head with my name carefully written in all capital letters, "CAL!" She had used a thick purple magic marker and there was no mistaking that this was my date for the evening. I hesitated for just a moment before walking up to introduce myself in person for the first time.

"Cal, Cal, Cal, this is Cal!" She sang, holding the sign out to me in case I forgot.

We went in and she showed me off to her friends. Like all pre-teens that have ever attended football games, they had no interest in the game. We stood in a circle on the path that surrounds the field and the track.

There were a few highlights of this night that seem more like a fever dream as I look back on it all these years later.

A boy came up to one of the girls in the group and flicked a lighter in her face. She had used a generous amount of hair spray and it caught on fire for a moment. Her friends patted her flaming head out quickly and poured a half bottle of Gatorade on it just to be sure. Somehow it was my responsibility to question him and teach this ten-year-old boy a lesson. I casually told him he shouldn't do that again. He explained that, at his school, he and his friends greet each other by flicking lighters in each other's faces.

The next boy to approach us asked me to speak with him

privately. I looked around, confused. Did this little kid mean me? No one at this game knew me and I certainly didn't know him. The girls were getting upset and talking amongst themselves in hushed whispers as I walked with him under the stands.

"Are you trying to move in on my woman?" He asked. He was surprisingly calm given the situation that was slowly being revealed to me.

"I don't even know what you're talking about. What woman?" I asked, utterly confused.

"She's my girlfriend. What the hell do you think you're doing coming around here?" He was starting to get more agitated now.

"Listen, I don't know what you think is going on. But I am absolutely not moving in on your girl," I said. This was probably the truest statement I have ever spoke in my life.

"That's good. Make sure you keep it that way or me and my friends will make you sorry," He made himself very clear and walked away slowly, leaving me in disbelief.

She came over just as he was out of earshot, "What did he say to you?"

"Jesus Christ! Is he your boyfriend!?" I asked, still trying to register what had just happened.

"Yeah, but don't worry about him. He keeps trying to break up with me. But he can't because I tell him I'll commit suicide. Let's go get some snacks. Brittany says you want to buy me a pretzel with cheese."

What in the hell did my mom's good intentions get me into?

We sat in the stands together when halftime started and

we watched the band. She told me about her bird and how it talked to her, but only when no one else was listening. I finished my candy and she licked the last of her cheese cup after she ran out of pretzel to dip. The game finally ended and I think her home team won. Who cares? I was just happy that no one else was set on fire and I didn't get shanked in a crime of jealous rage.

We joined the people who were bottlenecked at the exit and waited for the crowd to disperse. Her mom would be there any moment to pick her up and so I would have to wait for my mom somewhere out of sight because her parents couldn't know that we had gone out together. We said our goodbyes. Then she got much closer to me, leaned her head back and closed her eyes. She said quietly but very clearly, "Brittany says you want to kiss me."

Two of Hearts

There is nothing more satisfying than seeing two movies back to back at the theater. The first double-feature I went to was *Angels in the Outfield* and *Lion King*. While neither of those movies were very high on my watch list at the time, I loved the idea of seeing both films for the price of one.

Years later, in October of 2005, I had a much more mature taste in movies but my craving for a cinematic BOGO deal had not diminished in the least.

Some friends and I had left work early to meet for the seven o'clock show of *Saw 2*, a masterpiece of modern horror and really the only one of the series that I like enough to watch again.

We were used to going to movies after work for the last show of the night, but that night we found ourselves behind enemy lines with a theater full of new releases and two hours to kill when our first movie ended. Looking over the available movies to complete our double feature, I voted for *Wallace and Gromit: Curse of the Were-Rabbit* but was quickly vetoed as it wouldn't pair well with the horror movie we had just seen. We all agreed on *Waiting* with Van Wilder, he'd later be known as Ryan Reynolds but back then none of us knew his real name.

After working a full shift and sitting through a full movie, I was getting hungry. But I wasn't about to pay movie theater prices for snacks. I had to improvise. I snuck back into the original auditorium we had just left and grabbed a mostly empty popcorn tub, poured out the remaining kernels and bits of trash, and took it back to the lobby for a refill. I waved my ticket stub, obnoxiously, as I walked past the attendant so he'd remember me when I passed back through since I couldn't have him checking over my ticket again. I got a fresh refill with plenty of butter and napkins and made my way back towards the next show without incident.

Getting my food had taken longer than expected and the previews were already starting. I jogged down the long hallway and pulled the door open in a hurry. It was much heavier than I thought it would be and didn't open very far. When I attempted to lunge through, I smashed into the edge of the door and it nearly scraped my left nipple raw. I spilled half of my newly acquired tub all over the entryway and screamed out in agonizing pain. I stumbled to my seat in the dark, crowded theater.

The movie was hilarious and a perfect balance to the gory film we had just seen and the popcorn was more delicious than usual, probably because of the effort and determination it took to get.

We finished off the night at Perkins, drinking milkshakes into the early morning. We had a great night out, despite the droplets of blood from my nipple that soaked through my shirt and a terrible stomach ache the next morning. Best of all, "Nipple Jumping" was born that night. That's what I call paying for one movie and then sneaking into another. This name, without context, doesn't help when I'm trying to convince people who don't necessarily want to join us for such a bargain.

"It'll be great! We'll get our snacks and drinks out of the trash. Just make sure your nipples are protected!" As I lift my shirt to show off my single intact nipple and the other that is mangled beyond recognition.

Three of Hearts

Growing up, my family nicknamed me The Bike Killer. I used to dispute this. It might have seemed like I destroyed a lot of bikes, but in relation to the far distances I'd ride every week, I was going through the appropriate number of bicycles. I have recently looked back on my many accidents that claimed the lives of my bikes and most of them were my own doing. In hindsight, I now agree with their assessment that I could not be trusted with anything nicer than a hand-me-down bike from a garage sale.

I'm including a few examples below. I will only discuss the times that were – possibly - my fault.

My older brother, Josh, had a skinny-tire ten speed and he had just installed a speedometer onto it. This would include little sensors on the rim and on the bike frame that would pass each other each time the wheel would make a full rotation. Then a tiny wire would send that info up to a little computer attached between the handlebars. This might not sound overly exciting now. But, trust me when I say, to a ten-year-old in the '80s, this was the pinnacle of modern technology.

I borrowed his bike and immediately felt like Ivan Drago, training at his high-tech gym in Rocky IV!

I pulled out into my street and started pedaling with all my might. I watched the tiny computer screen as the digital number rose with each strenuous push. 6 MPH, 7 MPH, 8 MPH... Increasing slowly, then maintaining. Adrenaline was pumping through my veins!

How fast would I be able to get?

How long would my young legs last at that speed?

Does the speedometer max out at a certain point, like on a car, or will the wheels start to fall off from the extreme vibrations before I reach that point?

The possibilities were endless at that moment. I would be able to get to Dairy Mart in a matter of minutes. I would never ride in a car again. This was so much fa---

SMASH!!! Distracted, I had caught my handlebar on the driver's side mirror of a parked car. I went flying over the bike, the mirror shattered and snapped off the car, and my brother's bike was bent up pretty bad.

I looked around to assess the damage and see if there were any witnesses. I was scraped up, but nothing was broken. I scooped the shards of the mirror into the plastic casing and balanced it all on the front windshield of the car, flipping the wiper up so the owner would notice when they came outside. As if they wouldn't see the destruction immediately.

I then pushed the bike back down the block to my garage. This was a relatively short trip home. I had only made it four houses before the crash. The front wheel was bent out of shape, the handlebars were tilted all the way forward and, worst of all, the speedometer no longer worked. I hung the bike back up on the hook and went inside to clean the gravel out of my elbows.

My brother was pissed the next day when he tried to take his bike for a ride, but I denied any involvement until today.

One of my first jobs was in the electronics department at Wal-Mart on Brookpark Road in North Olmsted, OH. For reference, this is a very busy road with two lanes going each way and a grass island in the middle.

During that summer, (Probably '98, I remember the original Pokémon Red and Blue games came out while I worked there) they were doing construction all down the street on both sides. I was used to riding on the sidewalk on Brookpark to avoid the heavy traffic and was delighted, one afternoon after work, to see the construction crew was gone and there were cones blocking the outside lane in my direction.

I took this opportunity to ride on this closed road with no possibility of cars, either moving or parked, running me over. I was picking up speed and feeling the breeze on my face when I slowed down for just a split second. It felt like I had tapped on the brakes even though I hadn't. I continued on without a care or even a second to consider what was happening. Then, I felt that resistance again, for just a moment. The third time, my luck (and forward momentum) ran out. I had been riding through patches of wet cement. The first few were very close to being dry and looking back, I just saw slight tire track indentions. The last one, my tire smooshed down into the cement immediately and my bike came to an abrupt stop, throwing me over the handlebars and face-first into the muck. I pulled myself up and wiped the cement out of my hair and off my face. I must have looked a lot like Han Solo in Empire if he was an idiot on a ten-speed.

I pulled my bike out of the street and slowly rode home.

I didn't realize, at the time, that the cement was drying onto the bike frame and tires.

That bike was much heavier from that day on.

Four of Hearts

Jeanette and I had been married for about five years when she surprised me with the greatest trip of my life.

We loaded our two daughters into the car and drove two and a half hours to a shopping mall in Pittsburgh. Most people would say it's absurd to use a tank of gas to drive three hundred miles to go shopping for an afternoon but anyone who knows me, or horror movies in general, knows why we had to go.

Monroeville Mall is where George A. Romero filmed the 1978 horror classic, *Dawn of the Dead*. I first rented that movie when I was very young. I hadn't even seen Night yet at that time but the VHS cover looked cool and I wasn't disappointed. I've probably seen it thirty times and still quote the movie at least once a week. It's a fair bet that if I say something you don't understand, assume it's from that movie. I know every scene by heart from every different cut and have watched the movie with many different director and cast commentaries. I live and breathe *Dawn of the Dead* and all the original Romero zombie movies.

We arrived in the early afternoon and, despite my opposition, started our visit at the Mister Rogers play area. He's also from Pittsburgh and apparently mall management thought Fred's playland would be more appropriate than George's. The girls ran around the closed-in area and took turns on the slide while I marveled at the escalators and the JCPenney sign.

"Honey, look at that wall!" and "Honey, look at that parking light!" and "Honey, look at that..."

"Yes dear, it's all very exciting. And before you say it, we certainly whooped 'em, we whooped 'em and we got it all."

"We whooped 'em didn't we!!!" I yelled with the proper gusto, as I ran off to find more areas of the mall I recognized.

There was a black security guard on duty and I mentioned to Jeanette that we should keep him on our side if things got out of hand with the undead or with any biker gangs. She said I sounded racist. After thinking about it for a moment, I corrected her that I was just being nerdy. I had spent years watching Duane Jones as Ben (and Tony Todd in the '90 remake) and Ken Foree as Peter. I knew that you always wanted a black hero during a zombie outbreak.

My daughters were much more interested in the toy store than the access hallways or elevators but I was finally able to pull them away to check out the ice rink, which was converted into the food court by then. We got Charlie's for lunch and then went upstairs to Suncoast. I already owned the movie twice on VHS and both DVD releases but I had to purchase a copy from the mall where it was filmed.

The cashier greeted us as we entered the store. I went straight to the register assuming they kept copies of my favorite movie behind the counter.

"I bet you know what movie I'd like to buy!" I said with an awkward, overly long wink.

"Why, did you call ahead and have us hold something for you?"

"Um, I drove over two hours to get here. You know what I need."

"I'm sorry, I really don't." She looked my family over with a questioning look. She was desperately trying to pick up clues as to what movie I might be asking for.

"Dawn of the Dead! Dawn of the Dead! You do know where we are, don't you!?" I couldn't believe they would hire someone at any movie store who didn't know Dawn, let alone a movie store inside Monroeville Mall.

She searched for the DVD but to no avail. They didn't have it in stock but she could try to order me a copy.

I left in despair. We spent some time exploring the service hallways, hoping to find a staircase or boiler room I recognized. We went out to the parking lot and took pictures of some of the entrances and overhead lights.

It was a wonderful day with my family. They were all very patient with me and listened to my anecdotes.

But the best part of that day was years later. On December 26, 2009, Suncoast closed 150 stores. One of them was probably the stupid one in Monroeville Mall.

Five of Hearts

My friends and I had an annual party in our buddy, Zack's, backyard. The yard was a massive field that must have gone back a quarter-mile with woods on either side. We set up tents, built a fire, and drank. Boy did we drink!

One year, I couldn't find my tent and decided to sleep out under the stars. We started drinking in the afternoon and continued into the night. I'm not sure how many beers I had that day but I was known for bringing two twelve packs of Molson Canadian and working my way through all of them over the weekend.

The night wrapped up and people started toward their tents. I had passed out on an empty refrigerator box and it had started pouring rain. My friends were truly concerned that I was going to drown when the rain came down and filled my open mouth. They dragged me, unconscious, into my friend, Tim's, tent.

It's important to know that Tim had lost half of his tent poles so the back part of the tent was propped up as normal but it sloped down towards the front and the door was lying flat on the ground.

In the middle of the night, I woke up and noticed that it

was soaking wet all around us. I, at least, realized I was in a tent and that someone else was sleeping beside me.

"Why is it so wet in here?" I asked innocently.

Waking up quickly, Tim screamed. "Because you pissed in here, you son of a bitch!"

Apparently, I got up shortly before that and couldn't find the tent zipper. I must have been kind of confused how I had actually ended up in a tent in the first place. I had to pee terribly, and we learned that twenty-four beers will cover every square inch of a two-man tent. He claims that I had lowered my pants and raised my hands and he woke up suddenly to me hosing him down while making jazz hands and yelling "Woohoo!" I don't debate that I urinated on him, but I vehemently argue that I would never have done jazz hands. I don't remember that night, though, so it's hard for me to convince anyone of the specific details.

As he was yelling at me again, our friend, Tony, walked past our tent, "Hey Tim, I have to piss. Should I come in there or..."? This only made him more upset and started the screaming anew... And I blacked out again.

When I woke up the next morning, the rain had stopped at some point and the site was drying up, unlike my jeans, they were still soaked with my urine. I walked around the tents and saw no signs of life as everyone was still sleeping and would be for the next few hours, at least.

I had to pee again. I don't know how I had anything left. I walked ten feet into the woods and was proud of myself for having the composure to not have another incident on my friend, who very well might have saved my life the night before. I undid my wet pants and let loose. It was then that I realized Zack's yard was next to a golf course with a small strip of trees creating the border. A group of golfers rolled up in their golf cart and found a piss-soaked teenager with his wiener in his hand looking out of the woods at them.

I had gotten into enough trouble this weekend and it was time to go home. I found a pen and notepad in someone's car. I left a note and walked five miles home with those horrible damp jeans causing the worst chafing I'd ever known. Hours later, people started to wake up and found my note pinned under a rock,

"I gotta walk this shit off!"

Six of Hearts

My family didn't take traditional day trips like most of my friends did. We spent our weekends at Whipps Ledges in Hinckley, Ohio, or New River Gorge in West Virginia. We were always camping, hiking, and rock climbing.

It was a big deal when we were going out on a boat with my dad's cousin, Noel. Noel was, and is, my idol. Since I was a little boy, I called him Awesome Noel because he was awesome at pretty much everything he did. He would come over and we played basketball. He could hit shots from anywhere in our driveway. When we played pool, he was the only one calling his shots and actually sinking the balls on purpose. Also, he was hilarious! One time when I helped stain the deck at his new house, he pulled out his checkbook to pay me.

"How do you spell Templeton?" He asked.

"T, E, M, P..."

"I'm just joking. We have the same last name." What a jokester!

Oh, and he had a sweet boat, too.

I was in elementary school, probably third or fourth grade. Old enough that my favorite thing to do was skid on my bike and make fishtails in the dead-end street next to my house.

My grandparents were given the choice, when the city was building a street through our neighborhood, whether they wanted the street to cut through the woods to the street behind them or stop at a dead-end. They decided on the dead-end and that provided us with a football field and a short street for bike riding without worrying about traffic.

On the morning before our day trip on the boat, I was practicing my sweet fishtails. The church, down the street, had just built a beautiful gazebo on a fresh slab of white cement at the bottom of their back hill. These were the perfect conditions for picking up speed, racing onto that clean cement, and slamming on the brakes while turning the handlebars which would create a long skid mark, a perfect fishtail. I had to be ready!

I went back and forth to both ends of the street trying to get my rear tire out and around a little further each time. The last time (things always go well until the last time) I turned too sharply and fell over sideways and was tangled up in my Huffy.

My mom saw my wipeout from our kitchen window and came running out, screaming. She was overreacting. I was fine, maybe a tear on the backside of my shorts but no serious damage. When she got across the yard and into the street, her face turned ash white and her eyes grew large with fear.

I tried to stand up and look myself over more closely. I felt something pulling gently on my leg and noticed I was lying in a growing pool of blood. The large screw that held the back wheel in place was great for having friends stand on when we had to ride doubles, but not so great when I wiped out and the screw stabbed through my calf.

My parents covered my wound with a big bandage and rushed me to the emergency room. The doctors stitched me up and sent us on our way. The stitches would evaporate in a few weeks. I just had to keep it dry. That meant no showers and most likely no hanging onto inner tubes dragging behind speed boats.

We didn't cancel our day with Noel. It wouldn't have been fair to my older brother. We went out on the lake and I sat on the boat drinking Dr. Peppers while watching everyone else take turns riding the inner tube.

Seven of Hearts

Like all teenagers who grew up in the mid-nineties. I spent the majority of my time and money at the video arcade. My favorite place on earth was Aladdin's Castle in Westgate Mall. They had great games, the mall was never busy, and there was a cheap Chinese place in the food court.

One of my favorite games was *Two Crude Dudes*, a sequel of sorts to *Bad Dudes*. If you don't know that game, you have surely heard the amazing, cutting-edge voice sound effects "We're Bad!" The characters were much bigger in the second game, you could pick up any signs, cars, and enemies and throw them as projectile weapons, and it had snakes. I mean, lots of snakes. I would play *Two Crude Dudes* for a while but it was a traditional arcade game and was designed to kill you quickly and often, requiring lots of continues which cost too many tokens.

After I was done playing that for a little while and always when I was down to my last few tokens, I would make my way over to the *Klax* machine. *Klax* was an interesting game for an arcade. It's a puzzle game similar to *Tetris* which didn't really fit with the shooters and fighters that were popular at the time. It also stood out to me because it didn't have any music, just the sound of the tiles flopping down the screen. *Fwop, Fwop, Fwop.* That noise never stopped and still repeats in my head and haunts my dreams. You have to catch these tiles as they fall off the playing field and flip them down into a simple five-by-five grid. When you matched three in a row, they disappeared and you scored depending on if you made vertical, horizontal, or diagonal rows. Combos helped improve your score as well. Your game ended when the grid filled up or if you let too many tiles fall. Of course, they added colors and the tiles sped up as you completed more levels.

I'm not great at games generally, but I was extremely good at *Klax.* I could often beat most of the ninety-nine levels with a single coin. My friends learned this quickly and would leave me at the machine for an hour when I started a game, knowing that I would be right there when they finally returned for me.

The comic shop I was going to at that time also had a few games at the front of the store. There was *Narc* and *Klax.* The owner, Murray, held a month-long tournament that was practically created for me. Whoever claimed the most spots on the high score list would win one of two prizes. The choices were the *Narc* arcade cabinet or a rather large collection of rare expensive comics, five hundred dollars worth of books!

I thought about trying for the *Narc* game so I could destroy it with a sledgehammer and rid the world of such a terrible game. Or the comics would have been nice to trade for stuff I needed. I didn't really collect older comics but was deep into Image Comics, which was still in its infancy in 1994. I was looking for some early Spawn and Maxx comics that I had missed the boat on and had sky-rocketed in price due to the comics boom at that time. This was right before the comics crash that Image helped create and I, unfortunately, was an impressionable teenager and got suckered by the hype.

Murray was a savvy business owner and knew what he was doing. The game had two separate high score lists, one side ranked scores by top ten overall game scores and the other ranked the top ten per credit average. So the winner, no matter how talented they were, was going to have to invest a large number of quarters to fill up both sides of the screen.

I played the game a few days after the contest started and crushed the highest per-credit score on the board. If you make a big X on level eleven you can warp to level fifty-six for a huge point bonus. My name was in the number one spot! It was above another kid's name that was on the board all the other nineteen times. He was in the store, hovering nearby, ready with a pocket full of change to play again as soon as I was done.

I realized then that the other kid was going to keep filling that machine with money to ensure he held onto the majority of those leaderboard spots. With very limited funds, I gave up. I wasn't fully invested in either of the prize options and didn't want to get caught up in an escalating war of who could steal the most change from their parents' ashtrays.

Looking back on that summer, I do wish I had put up more of a fight. Sure, it may have been rigged to scam us out of our scant life savings, but that doesn't change the fact that it was a tournament for the only game I've ever been great at. This story could have been the only one in this book with a really happy ending. Woulda, coulda, shoulda!

Eight of Hearts

My friends and I gambled quite a bit in high school. We mostly played poker, with some blackjack thrown in if one of us was up quite a bit and would be the house against everyone else. We even played rummy for five or ten cents a point, which got interesting, and expensive, when we played up to a thousand.

Poker was our favorite though. We would play all night long, often till six or seven the next morning. We played "dealer's choice", so we had plenty of variety. This was years before the Texas Hold 'em boom of the early 2000's when the games started showing up on TV five nights a week. We were playing long before it was cool.

To keep things friendly and cheap, we played with a poverty rule. Everyone paid the initial buy-in of ten or twenty dollars and they were in for the entire night. If you ever ran out of chips - and most of us would at some point - you got to play for free until you built your chip stack back up. You were dealt a hand and hoped for the best. It wasn't easy to come back, though. Because without chips, you couldn't bet. You had to hope that others had a decent hand and confidence to bet and build up the pot. You could only sit quietly and swoop in to claim an occasional win and hope you had a good stack to cash in at the agreed-upon stop time, usually after eight or ten hours of play.

When we played "dealer's choice," each of us would bring a unique game to the table. Mostly different wild cards. Baseball is a seven-card game where threes and nines are wild, and fours get you an extra card. Follow the Queen meant that all queens were wild and whichever card came face up next would be wild until another queen came up. Seven bloody seven made sevens wild, but if you got one you had to match the pot or fold. Another game we played was high/low. In this game, you had to declare whether you had the best hand or the absolute worst hand. There would be two winners unless someone was ballsy enough to go for both. The different games added to the fun and excitement. I loved the variety.

Then, one night, someone brought up a new game that none of us had ever played before. Over the years since, I've heard this game called by many different names: Yablon, In-Between, Sheets, Between the Sheets, and Maverick. When we were introduced to it, it went by the name, Acey-Deucy. Ever since that night, I have affectionately called it,

"Screw Everybody!"

The game is one of the simplest games I have ever played. Everyone puts in an ante of a few dollars to start the pot. For this hypothetical, we will pretend there are five players, at two bucks per person there is ten dollars to start. Each person takes a turn individually as they get two cards, face up. Then, they bet any amount, up to the full pot, on whether the next card will be between those first two cards. If you get a six and a seven, or any two close cards, you can pass. As that gap between the two cards grows, so would your willingness to increase your wager. A three and a Jack, for example, give you pretty good odds of a winning card in between, so we would expect a bet of a couple of dollars at least.

This game gets dangerous, however, and none of us could have expected how bad things would get. Two facts led to the problem: First, the poverty rule I mentioned before did not apply during this game. Second: If the third card matched one of your first two, you lost double your bet to the pot.

One of the reasons I've always enjoyed playing cards with friends over going to a casino was that when one of us lost, the money stayed within our group. At the casino, it was possible, and likely, that we would all lose to the house. Acey-Deucy was similar in the sense that we were all essentially playing against the pot.

The first couple of pots went okay. A few people lost a little, some would win a little, then someone would get a three and an ace, bet the pot and take it all. Everyone would put in another two bucks and we would do it all over again. This went on for an hour or so and everyone was having fun. Then all hell broke loose!

If the pot starts at ten and someone bets it all on a sure thing like a two-king, and a king comes up, they owe twenty! Now there would be thirty in the pot and things would continue until the next "sure thing." Now, only two large bets in, and if they match up again, there is now ninety in the middle with no end in sight.

We ran out of chips after a few trips around the table and started using scraps of paper with IOUs written on them. None of us had very much money or jobs that paid more than minimum wage. So, when everyone around the table was in for a hundred dollars or more, we were praying to dig ourselves out of the holes we were each in.

Finally, our friend Brian won the pot and ended the game. I don't remember exactly how everyone ended up that night, but I owed Brian about three hundred dollars. He was a true friend and said that I didn't have to pay the debt if I couldn't afford it, but I refused his offer. I had made those bets and it wouldn't be right to skip out on paying. I didn't know where I would get the money, or how long it would take, but I would come up with it somehow.

The following night, we started a new game. Those of us who were down needed to try to even things out and the few that were up from the night before had to give us the chance to make back some of our losses.

That night's game started to go south in a similar fashion to the previous night. There were more huge swings and again most of us were down and owed the pot much more than we could ever afford to pay.

Finally, Steve (our friend with the most common sense,) made an extreme and logical proposal. All of our losses would be forgiven under one condition. We all had to vow to never play this damned game again. I, of course, was behind this plan immediately, being one of the biggest losers both nights. And I could only hope that Brian and the winners would agree to these terms and that my debt would be expunged.

After some discussion and deliberation, everyone agreed to forget the debts, we tore up the IOU notes and everyone agreed to never talk about, or play, the game again.

I held up my promise for many years into adulthood and

didn't play any version of the game until someone brought it up at a poker night with my friend, Christina, and her brothers. One of the players refused to participate. He must have been through the same disaster as me and my friends so many years ago.

Against my better judgment and shooing away the little Steve angel on my shoulder as he was telling me not to play, I gave the game another shot. This game went off without incident and ended rather quickly, thankfully without the need for any scraps of paper for IOUs. I can happily say that since that day, I have never brought it up again and have been clean for about ten years.

Nine of Hearts

Over the course of several weeks during the holiday season of 2015, I had individually raised over fifteen-hundred dollars at work for charity. The funds would be split between a charity connected to Call of Duty that helped military veterans find work and a charity called Snowball Express. They helped children of fallen soldiers.

GameStop held a contest to promote these donations and the top ten employees in the company got to choose between two trips. One was a trip to Infinity Ward Studios, to meet the developers of the newest Call of Duty game and spend a week behind the scenes. The other was a week in Dallas, where Snowball Express and one of my favorite actors, Gary Sinise, threw a Christmas party for the kids of military soldiers who had died serving our country. I didn't care about Call of Duty and Mr. Sinise's video announcement of the contest that they presented at the managers' conference in August is what motivated me to work so hard raising funds in the first place.

I had never heard of Snowball Express and had to look it up online to learn more about what I was getting myself into. While I was preparing my store for my absence during the Holiday rush in mid-December, our corporate office realized that it might be detrimental to stores to be without their managers during the busiest week of the year. They shortened the trip to a single full day, plus two days for travel.

I had to submit both a drug and background check. This was a first for me when trying to claim a prize through work but it made sense since I would be spending time with hundreds of children. I had received a few text messages from the event coordinator about my flight and arrival plans. She told me that once my flight landed someone would be at the gate to accompany me where I needed to go.

American Airlines is one of the main partners of The Gary Sinise Foundation and Snowball Express. They provide flights from all over the country to get families to Dallas. The travel expense alone would make this event impossible without their help. I heard stories of flights full of kids with no rules at all. Kids were playing up in the overhead compartments and sledding down the center aisle on serving trays. They had a blast and since they were the only group on these flights it was tolerated and encouraged. They didn't have one of these full planes coming from Cleveland, so I got ordinary round-trip tickets. But without any layovers, that was something.

When I landed in Dallas there was a woman at a special table greeting families that were arriving for the event. She was taking their names and directing them to the shuttles that would take everyone to the hotel. I approached her and told her my name. She knew who was supposed to be checking in at her gate and searched the list for me.

"No, I'm sorry. You aren't on the list." She told me, apologetically.

"I'm not sure what to do then. My only direction was that someone who knew would be here to greet me." I said sheepishly.

"Maybe text your contact and she can..." She was interrupted by a man on a golf cart with a bullhorn, a bright Hawaiian shirt, and a large sun hat.

"Calen Templeton!" pronounced incorrectly with the long A. "Hop on board. There's no time to waste!" He bellowed this through his amplifier as he shooed an old woman off the rear-facing seat at the rear of the cart.

I had assured him this wasn't necessary and that I didn't mind walking if he just wanted to point me in the right direction.

"Nonsense! You're the star of the show. Jump in." He was still talking through the bull horn so everyone around could hear and was looking to see what all the fuss was about.

I tossed my carry-on on the empty seat beside me and got on. I was glad I did. It was a very long drive to where all the arriving attendees were being directed to catch our busses for the last leg of our journey.

He dropped me off at another check-in desk and was off to get the next prize-winning attendee like myself. I approached the woman at this desk and again gave my name - and again I wasn't on the list. There seemed to be confusion since this was an event for the kids and their parents. She was asking where my child was.

"Well, my children are at home. I'm not..."

"So you're a volunteer?" She asked while already looking

past me at the next person in line. A woman that had her son at her side, she would surely be on her precious list.

"No, not exactly. You see, there was a contest for us to raise money..." I started to explain.

"If you don't have a child with you and you're not a volunteer and you're not on the list, I can't help you. You'll have to call a taxi." She said very quickly and had already moved on. It was very chaotic with children running around everywhere.

I made my way past the desk and found hundreds of families having a great time. They had a beach party theme with all the trimmings. Kids were in sumo wrestler suits, smashing into each other. A DJ was playing loud Beach Boys songs. A lady in a luau skirt and faux coconut bikini was handing out snow cones and leis. It was pandemonium!

Once the entire airport terminal was full to capacity, the president of the airline came out and made a short speech to the crowd, thanking everyone involved for their hard work making this possible for the kids and how he looked forward to a great week.

Everyone got in a never-ending line, waiting to board the shuttle busses. I was hungry after a long flight and hours at the airport. A volunteer was walking the line with cookies and water. I grabbed for one of each and was scolded. "Where's your child? These are for the kids!" After another hour, I boarded a shuttle with the others and a short drive took us to the hotel.

I waited in the long line with my bags, finally got to speak with a receptionist, and was ready to check-in. Again, my name wasn't showing up and they didn't know what to do with me. After some confusion and a failed explanation, I was told to try checking in at the volunteer room.

I made a trip across the hotel lobby and found a bustling room of volunteers handing out t-shirts and name badges. I gave my information, expecting more confusion and to be redirected yet again. This time was different, they recognized my name and called across the room to the woman in charge of all the volunteers.

She came over and, when she was told my name, called for the attention of the room.

I know that this will be the most unbelievable line in the entire book. But I assure you, it's true. Most of these stories are self-deprecating and I am too awkward and humble to imply that I deserved what would happen next...

"Let's take a moment to recognize the man who made this week possible! Calen Templeton!" (Again, pronounced incorrectly.)

Everyone stopped what they were doing, looked at me, and proceeded to give me a standing ovation.

"Thank you for all that you do. We are blessed to have a hero among us. If there is anything we can do to make your short time with us more comfortable, just let us know."

"Not to be too much of a nuisance, but I am very hungry after traveling all afternoon," I said as I took my credentials.

"Of course. Just head down to the dining hall. We are having pizza for dinner. Pizza Hut donated a hundred pies for all the kids. Go grab a few slices before everyone comes down from their rooms."

I skipped checking in for my room and hurried back across the lobby to where the tables full of pizza boxes were waiting, just outside the large dining hall. I opened a box at random. At this point, I would have eaten a piece with anchovies and green olives, anything except mushrooms. A man came out of the dining area and stopped me.

"You know this is all for the families, right?"

"Oh, I know. But I've been traveling all day and I'm just really starving." I explained.

"Yeah, it's just that if every volunteer took a few pieces there wouldn't be any left for the families."

"No, I know. It's just that..."

"And you do know that these kids are here because their parents gave the ultimate sacrifice!?"

"For sure, and that's terrible. But I'm not really a volun..."

"Thank you for understanding. And the poor children thank you, as well." He said confidently as he took the paper plate from my hand and returned it to the pile.

Still with an empty stomach, I found a desk in a secluded hallway and asked the hotel receptionist to check me in and give me my room key. This time my name was at least in the system with a reservation, however, they were out of rooms. With so many families that had checked in while I retrieved my badge and fought with the pizza police, they had run out of rooms.

I called my district manager in Cleveland and while she felt bad for the situation I was in, there wasn't much she could do to help. I tried to call my contact but, as I assumed, she was much too busy preparing for the event to answer. After an hour of panicked phone calls, I had almost accepted that I would be sleeping on a couch in the lobby when I asked the lady behind the counter if she had any other possibilities.

"I suppose you could upgrade to a suite. But you would have to pay the upcharge."

"I'm afraid to ask. How much is that going to cost?"

"Eighteen dollars."

"Are you joking!? Of course I want to pay the extra fee if it means I will get a room."

I was back in business. I made my way up to my room and fell to the bed, exhausted. Moments later, there was a knock on the door. When I opened it, I saw an attendant walking away down the hall and a basket of fruits, crackers with cheese, and a bottle of wine. It was included with the suite and definitely worth the eighteen bucks.

After filling up on snacks and wine, I made it back downstairs to a large activity area where the kids would spend the evenings doing all sorts of fun activities. There were two enormous rooms, one for teenagers and one for the younger kids. These rooms were essentially the equivalent of the Foot Clan hideout in the 1990's *Teenage Mutant Ninja Turtles*. The teenage room had dozens of big-screen TVs for video games, air hockey, basketball hoops, and even an official *American Ninja Warrior* course complete with contestants from the show offering advice to the teens. The kids' room had their own video game stations, pinewood derby cars to paint and race, and four bounce houses. Both had unlimited chips, pop, and ice cream. Everything a hundred kids could ever want, minus the "cigarettes, regular or menthol!?"

I started in the teenage area, found more GameStop people, and offered to help where I could. They stationed me at the inflatable obstacle course at the far end of the room. But no one told me that the kids would be racing through like maniacs and instead of sliding down the final slide, they jumped as far as they could from the top, about fifteen feet up. After catching some serious air, they came crashing down onto the midpoint of the slide, which would then bounce them, at a ninety-degree angle, out onto the concrete floor, practically crippling them.

So my job, in this palace of fun with no rules, was to scream at the kids to "Slow Down!" and "Take it easy!"

After an hour of being the sole Fun Vacuum, I was able to call over to an actual volunteer and trick them into taking over my post. I went into the little kid area and offered to assist on that side, thinking it couldn't get any worse than what I was doing before.

They had me work in the ice cream room, where Good Humor donated all types of ice cream concoctions and the kids were allowed to eat as much as they wanted. The only rule was that the kids could not take the snacks out of that small room as the organizers were worried about them dripping melted ice cream bars all over the video game controllers and other donated or borrowed items. That was the job I was given, to yell at everyone to "Get back in that room and enjoy your treat!" I made plenty of kids cry that night.

This was one of the best trips of my life and I'll never forget it. I talked with lots of kids and moms about how much they looked forward to this event every year. It meant so much to them to know they were appreciated for their loss and it gave them a chance to forget about everything for a little while.

I did get to meet one of my idols, Gary Sinise, and he was so grateful that GameStop had helped raise money this year.

He explained that many years, they had to scramble at the last minute to find funding or had to cut certain activities. But, because of GameStop raising money in the stores for them, we donated $500,000 which covered their entire yearly budget. In comparison, St. Jude's Hospital takes one million dollars a day to run.

I was very proud to be involved and it was then that I understood why the people who knew had made such a big deal out of my contribution. I was only thinking about my small $1500 donation. I didn't think about myself as part of the much bigger picture.

Ten of Hearts

I've taken multiple film appreciation classes throughout high school and college. While I love movies, I often hated those classes. I think it was because the teachers forced me to dissect every aspect of the movies and write extensive papers on each of them.

We also had to watch lots of black and white classics. I respect those movies but they weren't my favorites.

In high school we watched *Schindler's List* and had to write a six-page paper about it. I slept through the entire movie and didn't know what happened. I did watch *The Exorcist* the weekend before and so I started the report by saying that "Schindler's List was just like The Exorcist because the Nazis did crazy stuff and so did that girl." I then proceeded to write my paper about that possessed girl projectile vomiting on the priest.

This was the same English class where my friend, Tony, and I wrote a four-page paper listing our favorite, fake Rice-A-Roni flavors: Peach, Broccoli, Butter, and Chive! (all of those mix to make one flavor, not four.)

The San Francisco treat, indeed.

I did a similar thing in my college course when we

watched *Some Like It Hot*, a 1959 classic with Marilyn Monroe and Jack Lemmon. (Sixty-year-old spoiler alert, "Well, nobody's perfect." I just saved you two hours, now you can go watch *Robocop* again!) I had just watched *Homeward Bound: The Incredible Journey*. It stars two dogs and a cat on their adventure to find their owners.

I started that paper with "Some Like It Hot is just like Homeward Bound because..." and wrote a paper about three talking animals. I continued this for every movie we were supposed to watch and ended up writing thirty pages about that adorable movie.

I got a B- in that class with a note that said. "Never do this again!"

Jack of Hearts

"Jon Bon Jovi better come over soon and clean the poop out of my damn rabbit's cage!" Is something I never thought I'd yell throughout the house to my wife and three kids.

I grew up on Bon Jovi's music with my friend, Dave. I remember vividly taking him on a bike ride, we called them bike hikes back then, to a path that I found. It ran parallel to highway 480 through our city. It was about five miles long, fenced in on both sides, and paved with hot asphalt. The path was difficult to get to and dumped us off at a busy intersection of a highway onramp with no crosswalks. He sang, "You promise me heaven then put me through pain. You give love a bad name!" the entire trip.

My wife wasn't quite as familiar with their music but knew their songs well enough for me to get tickets when they came to Cleveland for the *Have a Nice Day* tour in 2005.

We had decent seats and were surrounded by die-hard fans. Most of them were drunk before the opening act was done playing. Bon Jovi came on and someone was screaming so loudly near us that it was overpowering, even for a rock concert. I looked to see who it was and complain to Jeanette.

When I turned her way, I was shocked to find her face a dark purple color. She was so excited and screaming her head off.

From that moment on, she was hooked and we went to see the band whenever they toured.

After about four or five shows (and one shrunken fifty-dollar concert t-shirt that I washed because I am such a thoughtful husband), we were thinking that we might finally be burned out on Bon Jovi. We agreed when the show was announced that we were not going to go. We held out on buying tickets as long as we could but eventually found cheap, nose-bleed seats at the last minute.

When we got to the stadium, we walked all the way up and around to the discount section that was practically behind the stage. An usher stopped us and swapped our tickets for much better, more expensive seats since the show wasn't sold out. In hindsight, this was the moment that would start the chain reaction leading my family to acquire a stinky, rotten bitch of a rabbit.

Jeanette had her fancy camera with her and started taking pictures as soon as we took our seats. With a digital camera and an itchy trigger finger, it wasn't unusual for her to take four hundred photos in a single night. And I'll just say that for an older guy, Bon Jovi is very photogenic!

The lady sitting next to us was also a huge fan and had also come to see the band every time they toured. She was trying to take pictures and video with her cell phone but they were all coming out blurry in the dark arena. They became fast friends and exchanged contact information so my wife could send her the pictures she captured.

They friended each other on Facebook and Jeanette shared

the pictures. I figured that was the end of their friendship and we would all go on with our lives until he came back to town at least.

A month later Jeanette told me that the lady posted on Facebook that she had a rabbit that they couldn't take care of and needed someone to adopt it...

Go ahead and reread the first line of this story and I'll give you two guesses as to what happens next but your first guess doesn't count.

Queen of Hearts

My good friend Dan shared a lot of my interests. We both enjoy similar movies and music. He called me on my way home on a cold winter night and told me about a cool DVD set in Target's clearance section. It was a three-disc collection of classic TV commercials from the '50s. An example of these would be the cigarette commercials from that time period where a doctor would take a deep drag and exclaim, "I love the taste and smoothness of a Marlboro, it's the only healthy cigarette that nine out of ten doctors recommend."

I was driving past Target anyway so I parked and ran in. Knowing exactly what I needed, I hurried directly to the electronics department and the endcap of discount DVDs. I found the one Dan mentioned and quickly read the description on the back of the case. It was everything I dreamt it would be and more.

I tucked it under my arm and looked quickly through the other movies on the surrounding shelves. No other gems this time, I returned to the front registers, paid, and was back outside in ten minutes or less.

On my walk back to the car, I saw a police car with its lights on. There were people standing around in the cold and it was surprisingly close to where I was parked. I approached cautiously, looking closely to see if anyone hit my car while I was inside. But I had only been inside for less than nine minutes.

"Is everything alright out here?" I asked the officer.

"Is this your car?"

"Yes. What seems to be the trouble?"

"Did you leave your kids in the car while you went shopping?"

Okay, I had two daughters at the time, seven and six. And a ten-month-old son. He was sound asleep when we pulled in and he never slept. I was going to have to wake him up and he was going to start screaming in the store. Meanwhile, my daughters were so bundled up, it was going to be a huge pain to get them both out of the car just to walk to the back of the store, plus they were going to want to stop and look at a bunch of toys and clothes. This was supposed to be a quick, eight-minute, stop. Besides I left the keys in the ignition and the heat on so they might not freeze to death.

Another customer was walking towards the store and heard my son start crying in his car seat. He had just enough time to call the police when he did see me around, which is amazing since I was only away for seven minutes.

The cop could tell I was upset and that my kids were okay. The guy who called was yelling at me from the other side of the car and the officer had to chase him away assuring him it was under control.

He did call me a knucklehead for leaving the car running which would make it very easy for someone to steal my car and kidnap all my kids at the same time. He also explained to me that since someone had called 911, he was obligated to write me a ticket. It would then be up to the lead officer to determine whether they would prosecute or not.

I cooperated and gave all my information. When he was done writing the ticket, he let me leave and told me that it wouldn't be decided until Monday. It was only Friday night so I would have to wait and worry the entire weekend.

But my immediate concern was letting my wife know what I'd done and that I might get arrested for child endangering. That probably wouldn't look too good for a guy working at a video game store with kids every day while I was also going to school to become a third-grade math teacher.

I couldn't believe how much trouble I was in because of my laziness and it all stemmed from that damn DVD.

I went to my parents' house the following day and told them about it. They were supportive and didn't see what the big deal was. We grew up in a different time and my brothers and I survived all sorts of stuff that would be questionable by today's standards.

Monday came after three sleepless nights and I called the police station first thing in the morning. I asked for the officer by name who was going to decide what to do with me. He had just gotten into the station and hadn't looked over the previous weekend's tickets yet. I told him I'd wait. He put me on hold and came back a few minutes later.

"Do you understand what you did was wrong?"

"Oh my God, of course."

"Are you ever going to do something that stupid again?"

"It was really only like six min..."

"Hey. Shut up!"

"Yes sir."

"Now answer me so I know that you understand very clearly. Are you ever going to do this again?"

"No sir."

"I believe you. Your ticket will be expunged. Have a nice day."

"Oh my god, thank you, officer. You too." I hung up the phone and immediately Googled the word expunged to make sure it meant what I thought it meant.

I was off the hook and I had learned a valuable lesson. From that day forward, I sent my two young daughters into the store for the clearance DVDs I had to own.

King of Hearts

My friends and I discovered a great, cheap place for lunch near our work. We have plenty of Speedway gas stations in our surrounding cities, but only one has the touch screens where you can order smoothies, fried appetizers, subs, and pretty good pizza, for a gas station. We called it Fancy Speedway, or The Drink Warehouse depending on what we were going for that day.

They don't have a seating area so we would often bring the food back to the office and eat in the downstairs cafeteria. Sometimes though, if the weather was nice, we would take our food down to the valley and eat in one of the picnic areas.

One afternoon, I went out by myself and picked up a pizza. A large pepperoni pizza was only five dollars on weekdays and so it was foolish to buy a personal pizza for only a dollar less instead of the large with leftovers for later.

I got my pizza and took it down into the park. There was a parking lot that overlooked the road and bike path so I could watch the runners and cyclists as they went by.

It's important to know just how crappy my van was at this time. I had gotten it from my brother's father-in-law for the cost of most people's single-month car payments. You could tell. The wheel wells were all rusted out and it only had one seat in the back. It had sliding doors on both sides, but only the passenger side opened without falling off its hinges. It was also loud as hell.

So, I'm sitting in my van ready to enjoy my pizza. I opened the box to find my large, very cheesy, very greasy pizza. There's only one small issue. They forgot to cut the pizza into pieces! I was prepared for some mess. I didn't have plates and very few napkins, but I could have managed if I was careful and ate over the box. This wasn't an option however with one giant fourteen-inch pie.

I attempted to tear away a slice, but sauce and cheese started dripping all over my hands and lap. Next, I tried folding the pizza into a giant taco. This seemed to work okay. It wasn't pretty, though, and I looked and felt like a slob. As walkers and joggers passed by in front of me, many glanced in through my windshield. They were terrified to find me, staring back at them with this giant greasy pizza hanging out of my mouth, dropping pepperonis in and around the box.

After a few large bites, I remembered something.

Months before, at my last job, we closed a store and I was able to keep a few things that were going to get thrown out anyway. I gave our toolbox to our next-door neighbor in the plaza, Moe's Burritos since the manager there was always borrowing it anyway. I had kept for myself the hammer, a giant blue tarp, and a box cutter. At the time, I threw these items into the back of my terrible van and forgot about all of them.

The only reason I remembered these items was because I had recently taken my daughter and her friend on a hike in this same valley. This was the first time her friend came out with us and we were taking her for a long hike into a forest that she'd never seen before. She was already uncertain about the trip and it didn't help her confidence when she got into the single seat in the back and found those items in the back, a hammer, a box cutter, and a large, human-sized, plastic tarp.

"I promise I'm not going to murder you and leave your body in the woods." If you were that girl, do you think that would have made you feel better or worse about your situation?

Now I was back in business! I reached into the back and found my forgotten box cutter. I'm sure you have probably never used a box cutter with a safety guard to cut pieces from a pizza so I'll tell you that it doesn't work very well. It actually cuts small holes into the bottom of the box more reliably than anything it would do to the pie. So, now all the grease that had been collecting in the box started dripping into my lap.

I savored a few more sloppy bites and then gave up and threw the second half in the trash. It was delicious but hardly worth the effort. If you enjoy your pizza from the fanciest gas station in town, be sure to check it is cut into pieces before leaving.

Ace of Clubs

I'm always hearing people complain that different sports are not included in the Olympics. Two that I often hear are softball and cross country. "How can they compete in so-and-so, but not my sport that clearly requires more skill and a lifetime of practice to master!?"

On that rationale, I submit a sport that truly takes guts, determination, and athleticism. It's called Butt's Up! and I argue that it's more of a sport than half the ones included right now, both summer and winter.

A quick explanation, for anyone who's been living under a rock for the last forty years. All you need is a tennis ball and a garage door. The game is similar to handball, although I've never played handball, so if the comparison isn't quite accurate feel free to let me know. Any number of players stand in the driveway and one person throws the ball against the door. It bounces back towards the group and someone else has to grab it and quickly throw it back. This goes on until someone misses their throw and it bounces on the ground before making contact with the door. When that happens, the player has to sprint and touch the garage before someone can get to the ball and hit the door with that ball before the person. In the panic, the person usually ends up smashing into the garage at full speed which is why no one likes to volunteer their driveway for these games. Amazingly, it hasn't come up in all the games we've played growing up, but I can only imagine trying to explain to your homeowner's insurance company when your garage door is busted off its track and caved in on your car.

If you don't tag the wall before the ball, you have to bend over with your head up to the door and everyone gets a turn to hit you in the ass with the ball. You may be thinking that a tennis ball isn't very hard and your butt is padded just for this reason so it shouldn't hurt too bad. You would be gravely mistaken. There is nothing more nerve-wracking than waiting to get nailed and hearing that ball slam against the wall beside you. At that speed, the door shakes a bit and you can feel it in your bones.

If you are lucky, most of the players will miss. But without fail, at least one of the throws will connect with your butt cheek or, more likely, one of your bare legs when you are wearing shorts. If you are a guy and you are thinking something terrible while reading this, you are absolutely right. Very rarely, when things hang just the right (or wrong) way. You'll get tagged square in the kibbles and bits. It doesn't happen often, but it is definitely something you keep in mind as you bend over after it has happened once. If you plan correctly it should never happen again.

The highlight of Butts Up! is when someone's aim is so terrible that they miss the garage entirely and the ball goes sailing over the roof. This is great for multiple reasons. At my house, that was where our dog, Chance, crapped in the back corner of the yard. Also, it meant you automatically had to kneel over. "You get the ball, you get the ass!" we would all scream in delight as they had to maneuver through the dog turd minefield.

My friend Tony and I would often bet on stupid, menial stuff. Neither of us had any money we could afford to lose so we would wager Butts Up! shots.

"Is there really an octopus scene in *The Goonies*?"

"I'll bet you five free Butts Up! shots you can't prove it."

"Damn DVD cast commentary!" I'd yell as I was forced to bend over and take my loss.

"Can you defeat the Vile Red Falcon and consider yourself a hero in *Contra* without the thirty lives code?"

"Hand me that controller, I'll bet you eight shots."

We had a long-running debate as to who could hit a golf ball farther. The catch was that he could use a driver and I had to use a putter. We talked about this often and finally decided to settle it once and for all.

We were at a putt-putt course with a driving range and we asked the attendant for a handful of extra balls. I should mention that I've never hit a golf ball before, besides playing putt-putt with dinosaurs and windmills.

We each agreed that we would get three attempts and we would take the farthest drive. My first shot went over the small hill that separated the tee from the rest of the range, barely ten yards. On his first try, he wound up and missed the ball completely. That counted as zero yards and I was ahead. My second shot was a perfect hit but again went about the same distance. His second attempt went just like his first, he whiffed it. I was going to win this bet!

I forfeited my last shot. I knew that I was never going to get any more distance with the weak club and thought I might be able to get into his head and smoosh the last bit of confidence he had left. He approached his last ball with hesitation. He placed his hands correctly on the grip of the club and swung with his best form. He connected and it went forever. I don't think we saw it land but it obviously far surpassed my piddly shots.

It was time for me to pay up, but we couldn't find a tennis ball at either of our houses. All he was able to find was a racquetball. "That's fine, idiot, you are going to miss every time anyway." I gloated as I took my position against his garage. He stood at the end of his driveway in his best pitcher's stance. He wound up and threw that rubber ball with all his strength. Bam! It slammed a few inches to my right.

That wasn't so bad. I just had to survive that nine more times. Bam! Bam! Bam! I was feeling more and more confident with each near-miss. I stretched my head back to ask him if he was even trying. Even though I had officially lost the bet, it was feeling like a moral victory.

Then it happened on his fifth try. SLAP! That little ball hit me in the back of the leg, a few inches below my butt. My hamstring stung like a son of a bitch and I screamed out in pain. Racquet balls are much harder and fly with much more force than a tennis ball ever could. I couldn't stand after taking that hit and so he didn't get to take his five remaining shots but it didn't matter, my debt was served and the damage was done. I don't think I walked right for a week after that and the bruise was enormous.

I'm not positive but I think that was the last time my friends and I ever played Butts Up!

Two of Clubs

Although I didn't plan it, a prominent theme throughout the stories in this book seems to be the games I have played growing up. I realized after a few chapters just how much time I spent in the woods playing some type of tag. One of the more recent variations of hide and seek we tried was at our annual cookouts.

My friends and family would all join me at a baseball field in the valley. We ate hotdogs and junk food, played kickball all afternoon, and enjoyed a hot summer day. I often tied these to a fundraiser for a charity that we were working with at my store that year, everyone would bring five bucks to cover the food and drinks and the rest would be donated.

As I said, the focus would be kickball and we'd play multiple games throughout the afternoon. Somehow, my son was a kickball magnet and would get smacked around by that heavy, rubber ball. I felt bad for him, but all my friends felt bad for me when Jeanette found out that her seven-year-old son got beaned in the head with a line drive while he was leading off towards second base. "God damnit, Jose!" could be heard from across that field and she would look up from the hotdogs she had cooking on the grill. That's when we knew we had to settle down a bit.

When the day started to wind down, a lot of people either left or passed out from heat exhaustion. Kickball isn't as fun without enough players in the field so we switched things up and went into the woods for Zombie Tag. Half the group was "it." They were the zombies and had to chase the other half, the "survivors." When a survivor was caught, they naturally became a zombie and switched sides to hunt the remaining kids until everyone was eventually caught and eaten. It was a good game because the young kids could stick with the older teenagers and still be involved in the action.

My two daughters went off down a trail with their much younger cousins. The adults and I played an intense game of tag which lasted about forty minutes. I was exhausted and had already been sweating profusely from kickball. Now I was a dirty mess from running through thorny undergrowth and mud. I'm not exaggerating when I say I would do anything to avoid getting caught. And it showed from my mangled hair to my stained and torn shirt.

Everyone was eventually caught by the invading zombie horde and we headed back down the hill to camp where my aunt was waiting to leave. The only problem was that we lost the group of young children.

"Oh my God. When was the last time any of you have seen the kids!?"

My friends just looked at me blankly.

I ran back into the deep, dark forest calling out their names in a panic.

"Ellie, Emily, Nate, Lilly, Caleb, Aiden, Dom!"

No answer. The woods were probably a square mile with steep cliffs bordering two of the sides. It would take me time to search the entire area to find them. That was assuming they were even still within the boundaries that were very loosely established. More importantly, I was praying they hadn't all fallen to their deaths over the sixty-foot cliffs.

At the far edge of the forest, there was a horse stable where they supposedly put on equestrian shows, but I've been hiking this area for twenty-five years and I'd never seen anyone use it, until that day, of course.

There were hundreds of people sitting in the grass. They were picnicking and watching horses and their trainers gallop around the fenced-in dirt circle.

I came bursting out of the bushes and into the crowd that was sitting quietly. The mother and teenage son sitting closest to me actually recognized me.

"Hey, you're the manager at Game Crazy. How are you doing?" I actually got this sort of attention in public from kids often, it comes with being such a high-profile local celebrity. Or, in my case, the dealer who sells video games to their parents. Normally I wouldn't mind but I looked like I just climbed out of a swamp and I was starting to worry that I was directly responsible for the deaths of seven of my favorite children, three of them being my own.

"HaVe YoU sEen AnY liTtLe GiRlS CoMe ThroUgH heRE!?" I croaked.

"Um, no. Are you okay?"

But I didn't have the time or the energy to try and explain so I hurried back into the woods. I can only imagine what they thought at that moment. I don't even remember if they ever came into my store again to give me a chance to explain myself.

Another thirty minutes passed and there was no sign of them. I gave up and was heading back to the pavilion to give the adults the unfortunate news that all the kids were, best case scenario, missing. But most likely, worst case, dead in the river at the bottom of a cliff. I was assuming the parents were not going to take it well and was bracing myself for some backlash from them all. Especially my wife, who was pissed an hour ago when she thought my friend gave our son a concussion. What was she going to say about this?

When I rounded the parking lot entrance, I saw everyone standing around waiting for me to return. All the kids were there, safe and sound. They got bored long ago and walked back on their own. They never told us and no one thought to come back up the hill to tell me. I was tired, cranky, and annoyed at the situation but I guess it could have been worse.

Three of Clubs

My wife and I got married when I was only 21. At the time, we were both still living at home. We spent weeks looking at multiple different apartment complexes around our surrounding cities. We saw plenty of terrible and dirty places and a few places that were really nice and clean but were way too expensive for us.

We decided on a comfortable building about a mile from where our parents lived. Being close by was going to be helpful when we needed babysitters.

It was a sublevel two-bedroom apartment and I moved in a few weeks before her to start getting things ready. Her mom was very traditional so we thought it would be best for Jeanette to continue living at home until our wedding day.

This was the only time in my life to live as a bachelor. And what does a guy living alone do when he has too much time on his hands? We hadn't moved much in yet since we didn't have anything.

I had a bed, a PlayStation, and a fridge full of condiment packets. I was living on fast food and Resident Evil 3. But those only kept me busy for so many hours a night.

I took my shower and walked to my bedroom without any

clothes. I wasn't going to be living alone for long and I was going to enjoy the freedom. When I got into my bedroom, I glanced up at the large window and saw my reflection. I was a handsome, but somewhat overweight, guy at the time. I gave myself a wink and slow nod. "Mmmhmm!"

With nothing else to do besides admire my impressive physique, I started to put on a little show for myself. I was flexing my muscles and blowing kisses at my reflection, savoring the self-attention.

At that moment, my reflection in the window differed slightly from my movements. It was difficult to understand what was happening until I squinted and looked closer out the window. The darkness of the night made my reflection clear as crystal. But anyone standing outside looking into my bright room would see me and my naked, chubby, pale body flexing for all the outside world to see.

It didn't help that I was still not used to living in a sub-level. Anyone walking past could see me perfectly without even trying. At that moment, it was a group of pre-teen girls who lived in the complex. I turned off my lamp and was able to see the shocked and horrified faces of those girls. I immediately wrapped myself in a blanket and closed the blinds as they ran away through the parking lot, probably as embarrassed as I was.

Of course, I didn't tell Jeanette about this, but she knew something happened when she moved in and met our neighbors. They were nice enough to her, and everyone loved our new daughter. I got nothing but nasty looks from all the parents in the building who didn't appreciate me flashing their daughters.

We didn't stay at that apartment very long.

Four of Clubs

My parents got me tons of gifts over the years. I was always very appreciative, but some of them stick out in my mind as being extra special. I'm going to talk about some of my favorite presents I received growing up.

We went to the Memphis Drive-In on occasion. Not often, but we never went to the theater so I remember those nights very fondly. (Head to the back of this book, under the Black Joker, and scan the QR code for the link to my stand-up about drive-ins.)

The concession building had a few arcade games, a crane game, and a machine that I was too short to get a good look at. One night, while we were waiting for the first movie to start, my dad gave me a handful of quarters and sent me into the game room.

He went to that mysterious machine and started turning a dial on its face. Every so often he would pull a large handle on the side, like an old-fashioned slot machine.

"Kerchunk!" spin, spin, spin. "Kerchunk!" spin, spin, spin... This went on for several minutes before I got bored and took my change and went looking for more interesting games.

The games kept me busy until the sun went down and the

movie was about to start. My dad came to find me and we went back to cuddle in the car. After the first movie, there was a break and my dad moved me to fall asleep in the back seat. As he was tucking me in, he turned on the overhead light and showed me what he had been working on earlier with the machine.

It was a large plastic metallic red coin that had been stamped with letters around the edge. **"Crazy Cal, He's My Pal!"** This is what our neighbor, Michael, said to me when we lived on Brown Rd in Lakewood, Ohio before we moved into my grandparents' house in North Olmsted the summer before first grade.

I love this coin and still have it. I couldn't believe it was really personalized just for me.

In the new house, we had a much bigger, functioning garage. My dad sometimes used the space to work on projects.

Every Christmas, I woke up at about four in the morning and waited until I was allowed to wake up the rest of my family. I watched TV. We only had three channels back then so it was always Romper Room and Mr. Rogers at that time. I also took this chance to count and shake my wrapped packages, trying to determine what was inside.

One year, there were two long skinny boards resting against the wall. They were far too big to be wrapped but they did have a large red bow tying them together. Looking closer and down to about eighteen inches off the ground, I found a wooden triangle screwed into each piece. My dad had made me a pair of stilts. They were so simple. He probably had the pieces leftover from another project. I loved them. But, unlike the coin, I don't have them any longer.

We had a creek that went through our neighborhood and disappeared into a deep dark sewer tunnel. That Summer, my friend, Mike, and I were on a mission to see how far the shallow stream went before we wouldn't be able to follow it any longer. We needed something to keep our feet and ankles out of the water and those stilts would work perfectly.

The plan was simple, we would stand on one while we placed the next, step onto that one, and move the first to continue into the depths. We made it two steps, tossed the second stilt into the water, and it was gone. It was immediately washed downstream. In our panic, we fell into the water and the first stilt followed its twin brother into the darkness and disappeared as well.

I felt really bad for losing them and don't remember what excuse I came up with for what had happened to that thoughtful, homemade gift.

The last project that really sticks out in my mind was built by both of us on New Year's Eve. I was probably nine or ten. My dad and I spent hours in the garage building a makeshift go-kart with a set of wheels, the size of little appetizer plates. He had plenty of spare wood and we used what we had available. It didn't have an engine but we secured a rope to the front and my dad, who is the strongest, fittest man I've ever known, pulled me up and down the dead-end street next to our house.

If you ever want to give someone a meaningful gift but don't have any money, try making something by hand. Trust me, I know from experience. They will love it for the effort you put into it and will appreciate it long after a purchased gift would have been forgotten.

Thank you, dad. I love you and appreciate you.

Five of Clubs

I had done some fundraising for different causes over the years. I was never all that great at it and wasn't comfortable asking people for large contributions. One time, however, I surprised even myself when I raised the most money in the company during a fundraiser at GameStop. And it was all for a chance to meet Gary Sinise, the actor most well known as Lieutenant Dan in Forrest Gump.

He works very closely with charity organizations for American military members. He was asking for GameStop's help to raise money for The Snowball Express. I hadn't heard of this organization but the prize for the top five managers in our company (of over 6000 stores at that time) would win a trip to Dallas, Texas the week before Christmas for their big annual party. When he announced this prize at our Manager's conference, I immediately told my district manager that I was going to win and she would need to find someone to watch my store while I was gone.

Snowball Express, for anyone who hasn't heard of it, throws a huge party every year for children who have lost their soldier parents at war. The way some of the moms explained it to me, "It's the greatest club that no one would ever want to join." I had watched a few YouTube videos of the event from years past and, after bawling my eyes out, was hooked.

My fundraising before this was mostly limited to a long-distance bike ride to raise money for MS. Every year I would miss the personal requirement of three hundred dollars and the team captain would have to swoop in with fifty bucks or so to get me over the mark. I knew that wasn't going to cut it and I had to get creative.

I started with my hot dog picnic/kickball game (2♣). It was an annual tradition at this point and people would remind me if I was ever late setting a date and sending out invitations. This event didn't raise very much money. Everyone chipped in five dollars for some cheap hot dogs, chips, and pop. After expenses, we usually had a hundred dollars, or so, leftover. Most importantly, everyone had a blast.

This has always been my go-to for fundraising and I wasn't sure where to go from this point. Then it hit me, I was only catering to friends that wanted to eat junk food and run around a field until we all puked and passed out from heatstroke. I had to expand my horizons! I had other friends and they preferred a different type of get-together. They wanted to drink.

I found a local bar that had a buffet and drinks for $XX per person. All I had to do was select the food we would offer and whether it was all you can drink for two hours or two drink tickets per person and then set the price. I debated for a few days over which drink option to choose. On one hand, we made more money with a two-drink limit. But on the other hand, I was thinking the people who would come out would only be doing it to get wasted. My dad was the voice of reason, "You can't get everyone shitfaced and then send them driving home!"

We put together some raffles and a lot of people came from pretty far away. The money poured in and now I felt much more confident about my chances of being in the top five. But, what else could I do to secure my spot and impress my idol, Gary Sinise, or as I knew him best, George from 1992's *Of Mice and Men*, which was also his directorial debut. This is when I took my love of raffles and playing cards and smooshed them together.

I think people buy into raffles and lotteries for one of two reasons. They either want to support the cause, like a fifty/fifty raffle for the high school band at a football game, often letting the organization keep their half of the money. Or, they truly want to win the big prize, and those people are sometimes hesitant because they know their odds of winning go down with every ticket sold. In the area my store was in, I was not going to sell tickets based on people's generosity. So I wanted to drive home a real chance of winning a worthwhile prize.

I came up with a unique raffle idea. Tickets were twenty dollars each. Instead of traditional tickets, you wrote your name and phone number on the face of any card in a normal deck of cards. The PlayStation VR had just come out for a cool $500 and was difficult to find during the holiday season. The winner would get the VR unit or a gift card for that amount, and Snowball Express would get the remaining cash from the $1040 pool. I started selling cards on a Friday and promised to draw the winner on Monday, not bad for a weekend of selling.

This would lead to one of the most stressful, panicked nights of my life. Tickets had not sold nearly as fast as I expected, and by Saturday night I hadn't sold enough to even pay for the prize. Was I going to spend most of the money we had raised at the bar on paying out this commitment!?

After sweating through a long, restless Saturday night, everyone came out to support my cause on Sunday morning. It helped that people could walk into their local GameStop, buy a gift card and give me the numbers over the phone since all the funds were going to be rung through the register anyway. (This was long before cash apps and the only way we could sell tickets was through Facebook.)

I sold all the tickets and a guy from the pizza shop in our plaza won the prize. He bought a Gears of War-themed X-Box One System with his winnings... Then he traded it in for cash less than a week later.

When all was said and done, I had raised just under two thousand dollars and won the trip handily.

The trip is a story all its own and the only chapter that I considered tacking onto this one. But to maintain the integrity of this experiment of randomness, I am going to put it wherever it is drawn to land. I'm sure you will find it eventually. Maybe I'll release a strategy guide companion to this book to explain the proper order you should be following.

Six of Clubs

BP was my first full time job after high school. I was a cashier at a twenty-four-hour station. I rang people up for their gas, snacks, and beer, made coffee throughout my shift, and did inventory on the lottery tickets and cigarettes. It was all very easy and mindless.

They could see I was management material and I was chosen out of all the employees from local BP gas stations in the Cleveland area to attend a class for up and coming employees who were thought to have leadership qualities.

The classes were held at the old BP building downtown and gas station attendants from all over the country were flown in to attend. Most of the out-of-towners were in their thirties or forties and had been working at BP for many years. I was only eighteen and had only been working there for six months.

The men and women from out of state were going to stay at a nearby hotel. I, on the other hand, was local and a short twenty-minute drive away. I didn't get a hotel room and was told I'd have to commute every day. This wouldn't have been an issue, except I didn't drive at the time and had to take a bus there each morning and back home every night. This involved a two-mile walk to the bus stop, a forty-five-minute to an hour ride into the town square, and a four-city block walk to the office building. Then I had to do it all again in reverse to get home. All while the rest of the potential managers rolled out of their comfortable hotel beds, enjoyed a complimentary continental breakfast, and strolled next door ten minutes before our classes started.

The teachers taught us a combination of BP-specific managerial duties and leadership skills, in equal measure. The only lesson I remember from a week's worth of classes was the story of a man who approached the customer service counter at a Nordstrom store in Alaska. He had some items to return including a set of tires. The cashier processed the return and the customer went on his way. But what is the lesson? You might be wondering.

"Nordstrom doesn't sell tires!" the teacher exclaimed.

The first day, I met an older gentleman in class that invited me back to his hotel room that evening. I obliged, I was a naive teenager, after all. I've never been able to read situations or people's bad intentions very well. He invited others but they all made up plans to get out of joining us. When we arrived at his room, he asked me if I'd like to sit on the bed next to him. It was a rather basic room with only one chair. He had something he was very excited to show me. Something that any teenager would be ecstatic to get their hands on...

It was then that he pulled it out.

A Sega Genesis with two controllers and a single game, NHL '94.

I was slightly confused but more relieved than anything. I hadn't played many video games since I started high school and I had never liked sports games. He was from upstate New York, where hockey is life and he was glad to have an audience to hear his thoughts on all the different teams. We played multiple games over a few hours and he whooped me easily each time.

Finally, he got tired and I left. I took the bus home, ate quickly, and fell asleep after a long day. I had to wake up early the next morning to start all over again. It was going to be a long week but nothing I couldn't handle.

The second day, I learned that the hotel my colleagues were staying at had a happy hour with appetizers and drinks. I didn't drink but always appreciated a buffet of cheese sticks and nachos. I declined my friend's invitation for another night of intense hockey action and joined the rest of the group on the top floor of the hotel.

My prior experience with alcohol was limited to small sips of my father's beer when I brought it in from the fridge for him. His plan to keep me from drinking had worked up to that point. I was little and curious, and he knew that I would find the taste of beer disgusting.

I had told my new work friends that I didn't like the taste of alcohol and they assured me I just haven't been drinking the right stuff. Someone ordered me a long island iced tea, light on the coke. At first, I had my doubts. But it was delicious! Frank the Tank said it best in *Old School* when he proclaimed, "Fill it up again! Once it hits your lips, it's so good!"

I don't know how many I had that evening but the group kept them coming and I kept putting them down. We drank as much as we could, during those few hours, until it was time for them to close the bar and we had to return to our rooms.

Which was fine for the others who were staying in rooms on the premises but I had to make it back home.

I stumbled through the streets of downtown trying to find the right bus. I must have looked terrible and smelled even worse. I barely made it home and passed out on my way into the bathroom in my basement.

My brother came downstairs to use the bathroom the next morning before school and found my legs sticking out of the small room, "Mom! Dad! Cal's Dead!"

My dad came down and slapped me awake. They gave me a ride to the bus stop since I was running late and hungover. Then they went out for the day. It was their anniversary and it was ruined for my mom. She was so worried about me.

The others were worried about me as well, they took turns nudging me awake because I had a terrible hangover and kept falling asleep. I learned that morning in class that I wasn't cut out for hard liquor and vowed right then and there that I was never going to drink again.

That lasted about six hours until the day's meetings were done and we all made it back to the hotel for that night's happy hour.

Seven of Clubs

I've always been good at math. Well, I was really good with math through middle school, before we got into the more difficult concepts that I had to keep up with homework to build those skills. I give my dad a lot of credit for this since we would go over math facts on long drives until I had the multiplication tables up to twelve memorized at a very young age.

In the third grade, one of my favorite things to do was a game where a kid would stand behind another student and the teacher would yell out a math problem and whoever answered correctly the fastest would move on around the room. I was very good at this game and impressed the kids in my standard-level math class.

I was so good in this class that my teachers reached out to my parents and suggested that I move up to the advanced level class. This would have gone more smoothly if they would have realized my abilities before the year had started and I could have joined the smart kids from the start of the year. Instead, I was pulled out of class one day and paraded down the hall to the class full of students who were known to be much more advanced than the classroom I was used to.

I wasn't overly worried however, after all, I was the undisputed champion of the "math snake game" (I'm not at all sure of the name, but that's what I called it.)

I only lasted in this class for one day. I didn't know about my Achilles heel until I took a timed test along with all the other kids. Any answer that had an 8 slowed me down horribly. See, I never knew to write an eight like a figure-eight. I drew two little zeroes, one on top of the other. I guess dad could prepare me for all the answers up to 12*12=144, but he never had me writing these answers down in the car.

The two-minute time limit expired and I had only finished about two-thirds of the page. All the other kids looked to see how the new genius in class had done... Only to be greatly disappointed. "This is advanced math, Picasso! Not a snowman drawing class!"

The teachers had learned their mistake and told my parents that I wouldn't cut it in that class. I just wasn't fast enough to keep up with the others. They put me back into the basic math class and everyone knew I had not been able to handle the pressure.

I don't think I was ever quite as good at the snake game after that either.

Eight of Clubs

There is no fear that compares to when you have a young daughter and she is hurt or in any sort of danger. My first daughter, Ellie, taught me this right out of the gate. When babies are born, it's common knowledge that they are supposed to cry, or else the doctor knows something is wrong. Our joy of having a beautiful baby girl was short-lived once we noticed the nurses and Grandma Sherwood glancing at each other nervously in the silent room.

Jeanette started to panic immediately and asked what was wrong. They swept our precious baby away, did some tests, and established she had a collapsed lung. They sent her to the NICU and she was placed in a plastic protective box that was pumped full of air.

Jeanette was having her own issues with the epidural they gave her and had to stay in a room for observation as well. I didn't drive so they put me up in an old, unused wing of the hospital. It was eerily sterile and quiet. That must have been the longest, loneliest night of my life.

I think it was the next day that they told my wife she was okay and could go home. She was adamant that there was no way in hell she was going anywhere without her daughter. We got to take turns over the next few days going to her floor, washing our hands raw, and reaching into the plastic gloves to rub her back lightly. She was so small and fragile that I believed we would never be able to hold her in our arms. She's a lot tougher than I gave her credit for though and she built up her strength and lung and we were soon able to all leave together. I was relieved and it was one of the best days of my life.

Jeanette's mom worked at the hospital and she was raised very differently than me and my brothers were. I came from a "rub some dirt on it" upbringing. If we couldn't see a bone sticking out, we were expected to suck it up. Otherwise, the three of us would have been in the hospital twice a week.

Jeanette, on the other hand, believed they were "better safe than sorry" and wanted to go to the emergency room for a cough.

Ellie was about six and it was Halloween. We were carving pumpkins at the last minute to take to Grandma's house. I was standing, scooping the guts out of her pumpkin and Ellie was standing on the dining room chair next to me. We have a fifties-style table and chairs with padded seats and metal frames. They have a little bounce to them.

She was bouncing in excitement, lost her balance, and fell, ass over tea kettle, off the chair. She started screaming and her mom instinctively grabbed for her purse and keys. I knew what was coming. We were about to drive downtown and spend the next four hours in the ER. We would certainly miss trick or treating and I wouldn't have three bags worth of candy to steal from.

I was desperate. I went down to where she was lying on

the floor, writhing in pain. She was clearly faking, or at least exaggerating her injuries and I was wise to her game.

"If you don't stop crying, we aren't going trick or treating," I said as a matter of fact.

She did not understand my logic and only cried harder. My plan backfired in grand fashion. We loaded the family into the van and headed to the hospital. The waiting room was as packed as you would expect on a Halloween night.

When we finally got to see the doctor and got an x-ray, we found out that she did, in fact, have a broken arm. Everyone in the room looked over at me and if looks could kill, I'd be toast. I wasn't getting any "Dad of the Year" awards that year.

She got to pick the color of her new cast, red and green. They did a great job of getting her taken care of and on our way quickly. We were home in time for candy after all. She dressed up as Simba and kept her arm in a sling as we walked down the street.

"Oh, she's a lion with a sling." People kept saying as they filled her candy bag.

We watched the videotape later that evening. Jeanette had positioned our video camera on the tripod in the corner of the dining room. It provided a perfect shot of her falling and the crunching sound her arm made when all of her weight landed on top of it. I reached for the remote to stop it. We'd seen enough and I dreaded what was going to happen next. Of course, there I was in the center of the frame speaking in a hushed voice. That was a high-quality VHS-C recorder, the microphone picked up my voice perfectly: "If you don't stop crying, we aren't going trick or treating." Just in case anyone might forget what I had said.

Our daughter was a legitimate Track and Cross-Country star in high school. We were in the stands for one of her last races of the Sophomore track season. She was on the opposite side of the field doing stride-outs in the grass waiting for her relay race to start.

Jeanette was watching her closely through the zoom on her camera and saw her sit down on the ground. She mentioned that something looked off and before I could even look up to assess the situation, she was sprinting from the bleachers and around the outer ring of the stadium. I think she could have beaten most of those kids in the two-hundred-meter dash that day. They say a mom can lift a car with adrenaline to save their child, well my wife could apparently run two hundred meters in twenty seconds flat.

She ran across the track, despite what the officials said, and was by Ellie's side. She called the coach and trainers over and she was soon surrounded.

Ellie fell and had somehow dislocated her kneecap. It was gross and looked a lot like Gumby's fat leg. The trainer was holding her shoulders and they all looked around the circle with concerned expressions as she cried in pain.

The coach gave a nod to the trainer and I knew what it meant. They were going to put a wallet in her mouth to stop her from screaming and pop it back into place. I had seen them do the same thing to Eric Roberts' shoulder in *Best of the Best*.

I was gravely mistaken. As I was pulling out my wallet, they called the ambulance across the field and loaded her onto the backboard. They took her to the local hospital, pumped her full of drugs, and finally popped it back into place after three hours of tests.

She was out for the rest of the season but worked hard in physical therapy and came back the next fall for Cross Country. She was stronger than ever. I was so proud of her and still am every day.

Even with the stress and worry that comes with having daughters, I don't dwell on what might go wrong. I choose to think of all the good times we share and the happiness they bring into my life. I often listen to the song *Father and Daughter* by Paul Simon and look forward to the adventures we will continue to go on together.

Look it up and you'll see what I mean.

Nine of Clubs

I've never been one for team sports in school. I enjoyed some backyard football with friends but never was any good at baseball, soccer, or basketball. I wasn't dedicated enough or naturally talented enough and my parents weren't going to spend the money or the weekend mornings to keep me interested in any of those sports.

The only sport I was really attracted to was Cross Country. And to a lesser extent, track, which I only ran to stay in shape for next year's Cross-Country season. It might be different now, but when I ran it seemed like no one understood Cross Country.

Assuming that is the case, I'll explain the basics quickly. You run a five-kilometer course, which is 3.1 miles. The races are usually at parks or college campuses and you run across fields, through woods, and up and down hills. There are seven kids on the varsity team but anyone can run. There would always be a junior varsity group and an open race as well.

I liked this sport for a few reasons. While it is a team sport, everyone has their own individual goals. They never turned anyone away. And it was a very social sport where the boys' and girls' teams practiced together and spent all day Saturday at the races together, cheering each other on.

I was an okay runner, usually hovering around the sixth or seventh varsity spot or sometimes dropping to one of the top JV spots. That was another nice thing about Cross Country, there wasn't any politics to worry about. You couldn't really suck up to the coach to make varsity. The times spoke for themselves. If you were on JV one week, you just had to run your heart out next week and get a better time than the slowest varsity runner.

I will say that while I wasn't the fastest kid out there, I probably had the most fun. I was known to talk to my fellow runners during a race, often to their dismay, and tried to encourage them or just talk to pass the twenty minutes that we were out there. Another thing I would do to motivate myself to be more competitive was that I would set my sights on a runner from another team that was up ahead, I'd pull out my "lasso" and make overly dramatic lasso motions over my head. You'd think I was in a '70's disco the way I'd throw out the imaginary rope and start moving my arms like I was pulling them towards me. As silly as it sounds and as dumb as I looked, it worked and I did run faster to catch and pass those kids.

After I started doing this out in the woods during races, another runner picked up on it and tried it the next Spring at a track meet. This was on the final hundred meters before the finish line, right in front of the parents in the bleachers. Then as he passed the runner from the competing team, he put up his hand and waved goodbye, like how the Roadrunner waves at Coyote as he realizes the ground is gone below him and he's going to fall off the cliff, "Beep, beep!"

He was disqualified for unsportsmanlike conduct. The coach couldn't believe he had done something so disrespectful and talked to the entire team about it.

"You should follow the example of your captain, Cal. He would never do anything like that!"

Ten of Clubs

We never took traditional vacations when I was young. My dad is a rock climber, so our vacations were usually spent at New River Gorge, West Virginia. He spent his days climbing with his friends and I explored abandoned coal mining sites or found a good spot in the shade with a book.

One of the climbing areas was next to a junkyard on the side of a mountain. Days spent there were a highlight as my brothers and I got to hang out among a bunch of rusted-out cars and find random garbage to play with. It's important to know that while other kids were going to Disney World or Niagara Falls, I would come back from summer vacation talking about when my mom found a frog and it peed in her hands, priceless!

Then, one summer, my dad announced that we were taking a trip somewhere new. We were going to drive to Canada, a place called Rattlesnake Point! Try to imagine the excitement I felt as a seven-year-old during the mid-eighties, G.I. Joe was my third favorite cartoon at the time, and we were heading to Cobra Commander's home base!

It was a four-and-a-half-hour drive to Ontario and we had to go through Niagara Falls to cross into Canada. I was excited to see the falls and possibly meet Destro in the same week. I don't remember the specifics, but my dad must have been trying to finish the drive with enough time to set up our tents before dark because we didn't even stop to see the falls.

"Look out the driver's side windows as we drive by!"

And we continued on our way.

I was so excited to see the mountain with a giant snake-head carved out of the top so I didn't mind. Think of a Canadian version of Mount Rushmore, but hardcore. This is what I was imagining and bragging to my friends that I was going to see.

This turned out to be drastically inaccurate and my first experience with false advertising. My naive expectations were far from being met. I'm sure it was a fine park; I don't remember much about it. Once I realized that it was just an ordinary nature park, nothing would be able to impress me for the rest of the trip.

I do remember a steep hill covered with loose rocks that we had to carefully descend to the climbing routes. When we got there and my dad was climbing, my brothers and I found hundreds of rocks with fossils, mostly small trilobites. I couldn't believe our good fortune and wondered how all of these were still lying around and not claimed by people who have found them before us. I soon learned however that getting the fossils back to the car would be much more difficult than I could have guessed.

Showing these archeological discoveries to my parents, they agreed that I could keep anything I was able to carry up the hill. Of course, I picked up as many as I could find and scooped them all into my shirt like a kangaroo pouch. This method didn't work out very well. I had to use both hands to secure my shirt and didn't have a way to support myself as the massive hill was too steep to climb while standing straight up. Plus, the small rocks and gravel made it very likely that I would slip and twist my ankle.

I was taking one small step upward and would slide two steps back down. Each time I lost my footing, I would drop a small rock or two. The rest of my family was all at the top waiting for me at this point and their patience was wearing thin.

Short story long, I didn't make it out of that park with a single fossil. They are probably still down there, some thirty-five years later, because no one has come up with a viable plan of extracting them.

After a few more days of camping and hiking, we headed home. On the way back across the border, we looked out the passenger side windows to see the falls this time. The following summer vacations were spent back at West Virginia and the junkyard. That trip taught me to keep my expectations in check and from then on, I was content exploring the old coal mines with a disposable camera.

Years later, I made a trip back to Niagara Falls with my wife. She got a babysitter for a long weekend and planned a surprise trip. She even let me get out of the car.

Jack of Clubs

I didn't drive when I turned sixteen. I think, at the time, I didn't want to have to drive my younger friends around all the time. As time went on, it became more about saving money and I really didn't mind walking or biking most places. I actually didn't get my license until I became a manager for Babbage's and my District Manager, Chuck, only gave me the promotion with the agreement that I would be able to drive to other stores, inventories, and such.

This was also around the time that we were having our second daughter. I was twenty-two and Jeanette made it very clear that she was not going to drive herself to the hospital to give birth...

Again.

One of the biggest inconveniences when walking every-where is that friends will see you around town and honk to say hello. Not knowing who they were, I would ignore them. Then, they would get offended and come to me later asking why I was so rude. This led me to start waving at anyone who would honk within earshot of me, just to be sure in case it was someone I knew.

Once a truck pulled up onto the sidewalk while I was

walking home from work. He almost ran me over and stopped mere inches in front of me, blocking my way. I wasn't able to see into the driver's seat very well but assumed it was someone I knew. I reached for the door handle, thinking he was offering me a ride and he slammed his car in reverse and drove away.

A few weeks later, we were at a Christmas Eve party with Jeanette's extended family. One of her cousins came to me and said, "You almost got right in my truck, dumbass! You looked so stupid."

There was one summer after I had my license but we only had one car. I was biking through the valley to get home late every night. There is a bike path for most of the trip, but the last half mile I had to ride in the dark street to get to the hill out of the valley to my apartment. I was slightly concerned that a car might not see me and I'd get hit. That never happened. They always saw me and jumped at the chance to roll their windows down and scream to scare the crap out of me, almost sending me crashing into the bushes on the side of the road.

Basically, Not driving wouldn't have been so bad if it weren't for all the dicks on the road. If you see someone walking, leave them alone unless you are going to offer them a ride. And don't be shocked if they say no. We've been programmed our entire lives not to get in cars with strangers. Also, if you honk and a pedestrian starts waving at you like a lunatic, they are just trying to be polite.

One morning at work, I was coming in from the parking lot when saw my friend, Vanessa, pulling into the lot in a brand new car. I was excited to congratulate her on her new purchase so I waited for her, watching as she pulled into a spot, parked, gathered her things, and walked the thirty feet to where I had been standing.

This was when I realized that it wasn't Vanessa at all. I had never seen this lady in my life. What should I do now? It was clear that I was waiting for her, standing in the middle of the parking lot staring at her.

"Are you waiting for me?" She asked.

"No, I'm sorry. I thought you were someone else. Have a good day." Is what a sane person would have said.

"Yesss! No one should have to walk into work alone!" was my awkward answer.

And so we walked toward the building, side by side, in silence. I couldn't think of anything to say to this stranger and she was clearly uncomfortable and didn't want anything to do with me.

This went on until we got to the front doors, which are locked and employees have to scan their badges to gain access. We had just been told by security that we should never allow people to enter who we didn't know if they didn't have their own security badge. So I took a few quick steps to get ahead of her, opened the door just a crack, squeezed through, and proceeded to pull the door shut behind me, right in her face.

Looking back, she must have been a visitor or a new hire, or a corporate spy. I haven't seen her since that morning. Which is probably not a bad thing.

Queen of Clubs

Twinsburg is a city on the East side of Cleveland, about thirty minutes from where I grew up. As the name might suggest. They hold a big festival every summer for sets of twins. The event attracts twins from all over the country and they celebrate with a parade, fun twin related competitions like three legged races, a full carnival with fair food and rides, and anything else they can work "twin" into the name. (Bingo turns into Twingo.)

This is a huge annual event for the community. It raises positive attention and funds for multiple charities and a great time is had by everyone who attends. Or so I hear. I've never been to a Twins Days Festival. I have a different personal connection to Twinsburg.

Whenever I talk to people who I hear are from Twinsburg, my eyes light up and I ask if they...

"Yes, I've been to the festival. The traffic is crazy one weekend in August every year." They often respond before I can finish my inquiry. They know this event is their city's claim to fame.

"What? No, I don't care about that. Have you ever gone to

the McDonald's at the end of the dead-end street and hiked back to the cliffs and the awesome caves?" I ask excitedly.

This truly has them confused and, I'd hope, intrigued. No one has ever heard of this place but my dad used to drive across town to rock climb there on the weekends. I would often tag along on his weekly climbing trips, but Twinsburg was always my favorite place. The cliffs were pretty far back in the woods. It was supposedly private property but I never saw anyone else back there.

One thing I do remember, for better or worse, was that the hike to the cliffs was always very muddy and swampy. If you read that sentence and are thinking those two words mean the same thing, and they might, it is not an exaggeration to use both. It was always a marshy, wet mess back there with ten million mosquitos that were constantly breeding in such a mucky, gross place. That's the first six synonyms that come to mind. But in case I didn't get my point across, think of when Atreyu's horse, Artax, sank into the Swamp of Sadness in *The NeverEnding Story*. (And for anyone who knows that movie, I'm sorry for bringing up that terrible memory. Go ahead and take a minute.)

After we parked and tied our shoes extra tight, we trekked back into the muck. My friend, Shawn, and I spent the day exploring the deep, dark caves and reading books. One time, we found a tight hole that went pretty far into the rock. With no fear, I started my descent on hands and knees. It was dark but I saw a faint light up ahead. My dad and his friends were climbing a route at the same time and heard a loud clatter coming from a pile of leaves at the base of the rock. Thinking it was a rabid raccoon, they grabbed sticks and rocks and were ready to be attacked when the vile creature emerged from its hiding spot. Right as they were ready to strike, I popped my little head out of a tiny hole that was too small to fit my shoulders through. My dad gave out a sigh of relief, both because he wasn't bitten by a wild animal and because he and his friends didn't accidentally bludgeon me to death. We all had a hearty laugh at that one.

I recently found out that the McDonald's was not on a dead-end street like I had remembered. We just met my dad's friends in that parking lot and carpooled to the trailhead.

King of Clubs

I worked for seven years at GameCrazy, a video game store in a fenced-off section of Hollywood Video. The only reason this is important is that our little store was in the front right corner of the store and the bathrooms were all the way in the back of the rental side which was the size of a grocery store. When we had to use the restroom, our two choices were to ask the Hollywood employee to watch our side or we had to pull our gate closed and lock the front door.

One evening this became a nuisance when my pants seemed to be getting slightly tighter. I asked my video store counterpart to watch for customers and jogged back to quickly check on things. Nothing out of the ordinary, so I went back to work. Shortly after, the discomfort was slightly worse. This time I wanted to investigate more thoroughly. I locked my front door, pulled the giant fence across my entrance to the other side, and hobbled back to the bathroom. To my surprise and horror, things had escalated since my last self-check-up. My right testicle was the normal size, but my left had swollen to the size of a grapefruit! This was quite alarming, but with no other option, I finished my night of work and drove home, stopping at Taco Bell on the way.

Once I got home, I explained the situation to my wife and she said that I should have called the hospital when I first noticed it. I hate the nurse's line. Every time I call for myself or the kids, they always give the same answer. "Drop everything you're doing and get to the emergency room, NOW!" Of course, this call was no different. Except, they now added that I absolutely can't eat anything (I knew I should have eaten my tacos before calling!) and I couldn't drive myself.

I changed into sweatpants, for a little more breathing room. My wife ate my tacos and called her mom to watch the kids and we were off to the emergency room.

My mother-in-law worked at the hospital which was both a blessing and a curse. Working in the lab, she found out her daughter was pregnant when someone was running the test and said, "Hey, don't you know her!" She was not happy with me when she got home.

But her job was helpful when I showed up at the hospital in the middle of the night to a waiting room full of people and the receptionist said, "Oh yes, your mom called in. You're the giant testicle, right!? You can go on back."

The nurses had me pee in a cup and ran some tests. Finally, the doctor came in, pulled a rubber glove out of the box on the wall, and blew it up like a big balloon. By this time, Ol' Lefty was the size of a mini-basketball, the kind you win at Cedar Point or the local carnival. He said that only happens for one of two reasons. First, the cord that your ball hangs down from can get all twisted up, holding the engorged glove out for effect. This will cut off the circulation and it will shrivel up, fall off and roll down your pant leg. ("Jesus

Christ!") Or, it's infected and you can take a pill and it will shrink back down to normal.

Fortunately, I had the second option. He gave me a prescription and it was back to normal within a few days.

The real loser in this story was the ultrasound tech working that night. He came into the room at one point during my wait with a rolling ultrasound machine and had the unfortunate job of smearing that cold jelly all over my balls and taking an image of all my business.

"This probably isn't what you had in mind when you went to school for this, huh?" I casually asked him.

"Not quite. Please don't look at me when I'm down here."

Ace of Diamonds

I think every parent has moments in their children's lives that they are not proud of. We all have examples of times that we lacked common sense and, in hindsight, are amazed that things didn't turn out horribly for everyone involved.

One of those times happened with my younger daughter, Emily. It was one year before she was going to start kindergarten. My older daughter, Ellie, was in first grade at the time. I was often responsible for keeping Emily occupied during the day while my wife was at work. I wasn't babysitting, mind you. Dad's take note, it's not babysitting when they are your own kids.

Our favorite place to go was the Bay Village Nature Center at Huntington Beach on Lake Erie. They had lots of rescue animals that we enjoyed learning about. The highlight, however, was a weekly star show for the young kids. We sat in the planetarium and a teacher taught us facts about a different planet each week. Emily got a passport and they stamped the planet that we "visited" each week. When her card was full, they gave her a special gift. I think it was a wooden model kit of a spaceship.

After some time at the nature center, we went for a hike

around the beach. There are steep staircases to get people safely from the upper parking lot down to the beach. It was about fifty feet down. We didn't venture too far down the beach often because there was a small stream that emptied into the lake. This was usually deep and wide enough to stop our progress.

One day we found some branches that someone had placed as a makeshift bridge and we were able to get across to an area of the beach where people rarely went.

The beach ended a short distance past the stream and there were big, jagged rocks in the water that splashed right up to the base of a cliff.

Looking back, I can't imagine why I thought it was a good idea, but I decided to climb that fifty-foot sheer cliff with my four-year-old daughter.

This wasn't the first incident I've ever found myself in, involving a steep cliff, and it surely wouldn't be the last. Usually, though, I had my friends, Tony and Richard, egging me on.

My other friend, Chris, would stay safely at the bottom with my phone ready. He would already have the 9, 1 dialed so he just had to quickly dial the second 1 when we fell and broke something. Although this seemed like a foolproof plan, my phone wasn't very reliable. I was almost certain 911 worked all the time. But I was the first of my friends to have a cell phone in '98, minutes were expensive, and I often fell behind on my monthly payments. It was not unusual for me to dial out to make a call and get an automated message: "Pay your GTE bill, dickhead!"

Emily and I got about halfway up before it became too steep for her to find proper hand-holds, besides, she was carrying her favorite small pink stuffed dog at the time. She was more worried about dropping that puppy than she was about falling herself.

I found myself in a dire situation, it was too difficult to climb back down and we were approaching even more dangerous conditions above. Not that it mattered at this point, but every foot higher we went was another foot we were going to fall to our deaths if we lost our grip.

I was making slow progress as I inched upward and then I would put my palm under her butt and push her with all my might, yelling as calmly as I could for her to grab onto any ledge or small tree she could find.

Finally, we got to the thick underbrush at the top of the cliff. The last obstacle in our way was a six-foot-tall chain-link fence that was meant to keep people from venturing too close to the cliff. We saw the backside of signs every ten feet or so that said, **"Danger! No Trespassing!"** Well, it was too late for that.

I tossed her over the fence and clambered over myself. We ended up at a walking park with dozens of senior citizens walking the trail near us. Many of them said hello in a confused and concerned manner.

We took the sidewalk back down the street to our car. I figured it would be safer that way. I suggested we keep this particular adventure to ourselves. But she excitedly told my wife about it the second she got home.

Two of Diamonds

I've gotten into trouble with my wife plenty of times for adventures I've taken my kids on over the years. The first time was when my first daughter was very young.

Jeanette had told me Ellie was allergic to cats since she was born, but that was clearly her excuse to get rid of my cat, Rose, that I had from before we got married. This lie would also ensure that we would never be able to get a kitten in the future.

One Sunday morning, when Ellie was only two years old and still pretty new to walking, we had to go to the grocery store. I decided to make an extra stop at the comic shop to peruse the fifty-cent boxes. The problem was that it was only nine in the morning on a Sunday and so the shop wasn't open until noon. I drove to a grocery store near the comic shop, three cities away, and we did our shopping for the food we needed for the week.

Then we waited patiently for the shop to open. We had now turned a twenty-minute trip into a three-hour, full afternoon. The time came and we were the first two in the store and I went to look through the discounted books while Ellie waddled around up and down the aisles. She soon found the store cat, Winston, and was delighted. She had never gotten to play with a cat before because she was "allergic" and she was going to make up for lost time.

I was paying attention, to an extent. I would look up on occasion to check on her in between long boxes. I was making a small pile that was growing larger as I worked my way through the alphabet. I wasn't so worried about my daughter since we were the only customers in the store. I actually felt bad for Winston, though. He was a very calm house cat and was not accustomed to being chased by young children.

Ellie, on the other hand, was just discovering a tail for the first time in her life. She was very intrigued by the noises that this animal made when she tugged on that tail.

I called out to her to stop and the employees were nicer about it than they probably should have been. I was halfway through the T's at this point when she came up behind me and said she didn't feel very good. I looked over to ask her to be patient for just a few minutes more...

"Oh my God!!!" Her forehead and cheeks were bright red and so swollen that she couldn't open her eyes. (If you are over forty, imagine Martin Short getting stung by the bee in *Pure Luck*. For those of you under forty, you can think of Will Smith's shellfish allergy in *Hitch*.) Boy, was I going to be in so much trouble when I got home.

I hurried through the last few boxes. Even during such a disaster, I couldn't pass on the opportunity to possibly find discounted Usagi Yojimbo books. No luck, nothing was going my way today.

Where was I? Oh yeah, my daughter's face resembled Arnold's when he took a stroll outside in *Total Recall*.

I paid for the comics and raced home. Maybe the swelling and blotches would go away during the drive home. Maybe Jeanette wouldn't notice. I parked and grabbed Ellie out of her car seat. I carried her under one arm and the groceries under the other, up the stairs to our third-story apartment. I was out of breath as she opened the door. She was waiting, ready to scold me for being out all afternoon for what should have been a quick jaunt to the store for groceries that she needed for lunch. Before she could finish her sentence, she saw my daughter's plump, splotchy face.

The good news was she completely forgot about how late I was. The bad news was that she was probably right about the cat allergy. I don't know what magic my mother-in-law pulled out of her hat that day but Jeanette raced to her house and they got Ellie back to her usual beautiful self.

Crisis averted. My daughter had survived her first experience with a cat and I survived my first, of many, knucklehead move with one of the kids.

Jeanette wasn't all that upset. But I wouldn't make it back to that comic shop for another ten years and I was sure to leave the kids at home.

Three of Diamonds

In sixth grade, our class spent a week at Mohican camp. This was a big deal for me at that age because, while I had spent plenty of weekends camping with my dad and brothers, we were going to be sleeping in cabins and eating in a giant mess hall. This was nothing like the tents and food cooked over a fire that I was accustomed to.

Immediately, when I arrived and was unpacking my duffle bag, I found my new camera was missing. Someone must have stolen it, during the bus trip, and thrown it in the pond. The week went on as expected, without incident. We went on hikes, climbed the fire tower, stayed up too late, and other rites of passage for a kid's first weeklong camping trip.

On the last night, someone had left their underwear on the steps on the way upstairs to the showers and everyone, including me, made a big deal out of that.

"What an idiot!" and "How do you not notice they are missing!?" and similar taunts were yelled for the entire cabin to hear. Someone gathered the courage to pick them up by the waistband with the end of a long stick and swung them around. They went flying down the stairs and landed at the counselor's feet. Not amused, he picked them up to investigate. Of course, he found **CALEN T** written in bold, block letters on the tag. He called out to Calen (with a long A, which everyone assumes is a girl's name and no one ever called me by my full name beside my mom.) The other boys were snickering and I had to sheepishly reach out for my discarded tighty-whities.

We boarded the bus and I slept the entire trip home. When I told my mom about my new camera being thrown in the pond, she was pissed and ready to call the principal to complain. As she was picking up the receiver, I found the camera at the bottom of my bag, wrapped in some unused extra clothes with a full roll of film still inside.

My cousin, Manny, is one year younger than me and would be going with his sixth-grade class the following year. I don't remember if I just wanted to sound cool and impress him, but I did tell him how lame the place was, how crappy the food was, how jerks were always throwing cameras in the pond, and about gross underwear being left by the second-floor showers.

He, naturally, told his mom all of this and that I had been the one telling him these stories and I got in trouble for filling his head with doubt and apprehension about the trip.

Around that same time, I got in trouble for teaching him the Baseball Diarrhea song, "When you're sliding into first And your pants begin to burst..." I'm sure my aunt loved that we talked so much during those formative years.

Oh, but I did make him a rad mix tape with ninety minutes of the best Motley Crue, Guns 'N Roses, and Weird Al songs on it. That tape was sweet! He might still have it if you want him to make you a copy.

Four of Diamonds

My first sleepover was over at my best friend's house. His name was Mike and our other friend, Bobby, came over as well.

I was seven years old and we rented the werewolf movie, *Silver Bullet,* with Corey Haim and Gary Busey. It's still one of my favorite horror movies and it scared the hell out of me at the time. The jump scare at the end made me hit the ceiling. I won't watch it with my son, Nate, though. He still thinks the "Hee-haw, hee-haw, he-always calls me that!" joke is a dad original and I'd like to keep taking credit for that.

During the movie, Mike's mom put out tons of pizza, snacks, and drinks. She didn't know what we liked so she spoiled us by getting everything the store had in stock. We never got to drink pop at home and I wasn't going to pass on this golden opportunity to enjoy these sugary, fizzy drinks. The other kids picked their favorite flavors but I couldn't decide on just one so I mixed them all together in the biggest cup in the house. They thought it was funny and it seemed like a good idea at the time. What was the worst that could happen?

That night, we tested out two experiments that we probably heard about on the playground at recess or on *Mr. Wizard's World*. First, we held a big magnet up to the side of his TV in the basement. "Oh, honey. He's teasing. Nobody has two television sets." Well, that was true after we were done. Next, we put a metal fork in the microwave and were delighted when blue sparks started coming out of it like a terminator was about to appear from the future. His mom heard the electric pops and came running into the kitchen.

"Alright, boys. That's enough of that. Get into the living room and watch some TV."

We watched reruns of *American Gladiators* that played for a few hours on Saturday nights. We got a little rowdy watching the events play out, but we were limited to what games we could imitate in Mike's living room. Joust was perfect though. We stood on the couch with our pillows and started whacking each other over the head with them. This went on for a few minutes until one of us hit Bobby across the face and the tiny zipper on the end scratched his eyeball. He made a big deal out of it and there was a worry that his vision might be damaged permanently. He lived around the corner so his mom was called in the middle of the night and she came to pick him up.

When he was gone, it was just the two of us left. We laid our sleeping bags out and slept on the living room floor. A few hours later, it must have been around three a.m. and I woke from a sound sleep. I felt really sick and had to hurry to the bathroom. I was confused in the dark, strange house and ran towards what I thought was the kitchen that would lead to the bathroom. I realized at the last possible moment that

I had gone the wrong way. Instead of the kitchen, I had run straight to the front door.

I was confused and scared. Mostly though, I was nauseous. I was starting to turn back towards the other end of the house but couldn't hold it in any longer. I projectile vomited a combination of half-digested pizza, skittles, and five different types of pop.

The awful noise woke Mike up and he ran upstairs to get his parents for help. They came downstairs to a terrible mess. And I was curled up in the fetal position right in the middle of it all.

His mom called my dad to come get me and then started cleaning the chunks out of the carpet.

Our first attempt at a sleepover didn't turn out very well but his mom was surprisingly understanding and we would have many more over the years. His mom never did get us pop again after that night though.

Five of Diamonds

It was 1979 and my mom was pregnant with me. My brother, Josh, was four years old at that time and my younger brother, Andy, wouldn't be here for another four years after me. They both had ordinary, traditional names.

When they were planning for my arrival, my parents debated long and hard over my name. My dad's first choice was Huckleberry. He was always a big fan of Mark Twain. My mom vetoed that but compromised with Thomas as my middle name, after Tom Sawyer. I sometimes wonder how my life would have been different with an unusual name like Huckleberry, Huck for short.

My mom liked the name Cal but not Calvin. She came up with Calen, which sounds fine if you pronounce it correctly. The problem is that no one has ever read it correctly as it is written. The E makes them think the A should be long like in Cave, when really it should be short, like Alex.

All my life teachers would read it on the attendance list and when I raised my hand, they looked at me quizzically. They always expected a girl by my name. I still get emails at work from both clients and employees from other departments addressed to Miss or Mrs. Templeton. It does make it easier to spot junk mail just by reading the outside of the envelope. "Mrs. Templeton, Open immediately for great offers on your next makeup purchase!"

I'm used to it now, but the seventh grade was the worst year for this. Middle school years are already difficult for everyone. We were all trying to find out who we were and everyone at school expected me to be a girl based on my name as it was written.

This was also the time I had to start using deodorant. At the time I thought Speedstick must have been really expensive because my mom wouldn't buy me any from the drug store. She did find a stick at a garage sale and I took it to school for the locker room after gym class. I didn't know what deodorant was supposed to look or smell like but the cap was peach-colored and it had a picture of different fruits on the label. It didn't say it was for females but it was implied.

It was mandatory that we wore it and so I caked it on my underarms and thought I smelled pretty good.

Seventh was also the first year for Track & Field and the school offered free physical exams for upcoming athletes. All the boys were scheduled before lunch but my appointment was for the second half of the day.

They had a hallway blocked off with hanging tarps with doctors giving examinations in makeshift rooms. I pushed the tarp aside and went back for my exam. And the place went crazy! There were girls in their underwear, shying behind anything they could find to cover themselves. I was quickly shooed away by one of the female doctors.

As embarrassed as I'm sure the girls were, it could not have been as traumatizing for them as it was for me. The adults made a big deal out of me coming at the girls' scheduled time. This was clearly someone else's fault, however. I didn't sign myself up for a specific time and was just doing what I was told.

They had to make a special time slot for me after all the girls were done. A male doctor made another trip back to the school. He was clearly annoyed that his day wasn't done and he had to do one last physical for the sweetest smelling boy in the school.

.

Six of Diamonds

My first job out of high school was at a BP gas station. I often worked the graveyard shift and the late-night customers were very interesting. The employee who worked most nights and trained me was an older guy named Bob. He kept a metal baseball bat behind the counter to chase off ne'er-do wells. He named it B.A.T. for Bad Ass Thumper!

I didn't bring my own bat as my biggest concern was never armed burglary, but boredom. I kept a stockpile of paperback books, from Goodwill across the street, behind the register for the nine-hour shifts with only the occasional customer. The day shift employees finally got sick of my British Petroleum Library and threw all my books away.

I wouldn't be bored for very long though. My best friend, Dave, lived down the street and would come to visit during many of the late nights when I was working. I would never know if or when he'd show up, but I would soon hear the cars honking as they swerved through the dark, quiet intersection. If you grew up in the late nineties, you probably remember the soccer balls that were sold at BP's across the country. They were everywhere. They had the green BP logo printed on some pentagons and different country's flags on others.

These balls were kept in big open cages around the front of our small store. That is, until Dave snuck up to the building, grabbed them, and started lobbing them into the surrounding streets. I would spend the next hour running through the streets, and into surrounding parking lots, to gather as many as I could.

Another fun thing we tried during one of these late nights was to buy scratch-off lottery tickets. Now, we didn't have any money for these tickets, but we figured that we would use the winnings to pay for the actual tickets. This foolproof plan would work similarly to how we got our drinks. That summer, Pepsi had "buy one get one free" coupons typed on the bottom of random caps. If you looked from the side of the bottle just so, you were able to see half a letter of the winning codes. We'd unspin the cap, throw it in the Pepsi envelope and enjoy our free drinks. It worked so well, what could possibly go wrong?

If you know anything about how a state lottery works, you already know how this is going to go horribly for us. There are far more losing tickets than winners.

We started scratching a few at a time. We would usually lose and we were keeping a tally of how much we owed the register. No problem, just scratch a few more. Occasionally, we would find winners to help chip away at our deficit, but those were few and far between.

We needed to make bigger moves. We started scratching two- and five-dollar tickets, thinking that when we won, we would win more and cut down our losses faster. This went on for a few hours and we had a small pile of winners but were down around fifty or sixty bucks.

I'm sure you've heard the expression, "Go big or go home!" Well, Dave went home. I was left alone and realized that while "We" were having fun scratching all the tickets, I was the one who ultimately had a job to worry about and would be the only one to answer for the ticket shortage when the manager arrived in the morning to do the daily inventory of cigarettes and lottery tickets.

I had accepted my fate and that I was probably less than an hour from being fired when I scratched one of the large twenty-dollar tickets. I didn't think it mattered at this point whether I was short sixty or eighty dollars. I went in for all the glory, it was all or nothing. That's when a miracle happened. I actually hit. A one-hundred-dollar winner! I had enough winning tickets to break even with a little extra for breakfast. There was only one more problem, the lottery machine wouldn't let you scan or cash winning tickets from midnight to six, which is when the morning manager generally showed up for his shift.

His name was Brent and had worked for BP for the last two hundred years or so. He arrived a few minutes early, as he always did, and started his morning routine. He would clock in, make his coffee, and head to the office for some administrative work.

Within twenty minutes he would be back up front with his clipboard to complete his morning counts.

I scanned those tickets like a squirrel on crack. I rang all the tickets out and prayed I had kept my tallies and done my math correctly.

Everything worked out alright that morning. All the counts checked out, and no one was the wiser. And I learned not to push my luck with the lottery ever again. I will still buy a ticket when I have an extra dollar, but I learned to never ever buy them on credit.

Seven of Diamonds

I'm not sure if I named the many games I played, growing up, after me, as a conceited attempt to slap my name on everything or if others came up with the names because they knew that no one could ever be expected to take part in our dumb games with such enthusiasm, bordering on ferocity.

Regardless, we grew up playing Jail Break in the neighborhood in elementary school which morphed into Catch Cal since no one else wanted to run away.

Catch Cal is really as simple as it sounds. However many people were playing, everyone gave me five or ten minutes to run into the woods, and then they would give chase. It was an anything-goes manhunt. There are no winners or losers in this game, or any that we played. It would eventually end when they caught me, but there were always plenty of injuries and strategies to discuss when we were finished.

One of our favorite places to play was Huntington Beach on Lake Erie. There was an upper picnic area with a playground and the sandy beach below, with plenty of staircases up the cliff in between.

At the height of its popularity, we were playing after work with the staff at Babbage's (Before it, along with Software Etc. and Funcoland were all rebranded as GameStop) and their friends. The store manager was one of my best friends at the time, Richard. He actually hired me on 9/8/99, the day before the Sega Dreamcast launch, to open systems out of their packing boxes and stack them in the office. Things were quite different back then with plenty of systems available for anyone who wanted one, but I digress.

One particular night we had more people than normal. A part-time employee brought a foreign exchange student who spoke broken English. I don't know what country she was from, but she was beautiful and everyone in the group was eager to impress her.

Everyone was gathered in the parking lot, milling around, waiting for me to run off into the night with my brief head start. The urge to pass gas hit me suddenly, but I held out until I was far enough away that no one would hear. The term crop dusting would not be popularized until much later, but that thought had also crossed my mind. Thinking I was far enough away, I let it rip. I couldn't let that slow me down. And either I wasn't quite as far away as I thought or foreigners have very good hearing.

"Did he just fart!?" She asked in her strong European accent.

This was followed by billowing laughter from everyone as I ran off into the night.

That round had gone off without incident. Then our friend, Richard, suggested that we mix things up and we play Catch Richard. He was equally motivated and ready to evade capture for as long as possible. We gave him the usual amount of time to find a hiding place and plan his strategy. When we started after him, he was just standing there in the open, confident in his speed and ability to outmaneuver us. He made it about eight steps in a full sprint when he ran right into an old rusty grill! More accurately, his watch caught the side handle of the grill and he somehow did a full flip over it. This gave him a terrible cut, from his wrist up to his elbow. He was bleeding everywhere yet remained much calmer than the rest of us.

My girlfriend, Jeanette, was there (Spoiler: she would become my wife in a few years) and had to drive his car home or to the hospital, I don't really remember. It was a stressful drive because Richard is very tall and had broken his driver's seat in the furthest position from the steering wheel. Jeanette, on the other hand, is very short, probably eighteen inches shorter than him. It definitely looked like when the Muppets would drive and one was pushing the pedals while the other handled the steering wheel.

We got him to a doctor and he got stitched up. He does have a nasty scar, however. I'm sure he has made up a better story over the years about how he got that scar. He probably doesn't like explaining how he got his ass kicked by a grill. But now you know what really happened.

Eight of
Diamonds

Pedal to the Point was an annual, one-hundred-and-fifty-mile bike ride over the hottest weekend in August.

Participants raised money for multiple sclerosis and rode seventy-five miles out to Sandusky, Ohio (home of Cedar Point amusement park, America's Roller Coast) on Saturday and then back on Sunday. I had never done it as a teenager but always wanted to try it every summer when I saw posters and flyers advertising the event in local businesses.

When my daughter was in school, her friend's dad put together a team every year with people from his work. I jumped at the chance to join and invited myself to tag along with them. I wasn't worried about the miles, I just never thought I would be able to raise the three-hundred-dollar minimum donation needed to join. This team was the perfect opportunity for me to enter. They had been doing the event for years, held a successful fundraiser at a nearby bar, and I would have people that I knew during the ride.

I started to train heavily two months before the ride and raised the funds I needed, with a boost from an anonymous donor on the last day before the deadline (It was the captain of our team.) I was ready. I even got a matching jersey with the rest of the group.

I was lacking one key ingredient, however. A decent bike that could handle such a long distance. My bike was a hybrid. It was kind of old but really not that bad. I got my eyes on the rest of the teams' bikes that were all sleek, light road bikes. All with price tags starting at two thousand dollars, and those prices went up fast. I'd be lying if I said I wasn't extremely jealous. I couldn't even scrape up enough money for the entrance fee and these guys had bikes that were, at minimum, four times more expensive than my van. (I wish this was an exaggeration, but my van was only five hundred bucks.

As luck would have it, an elderly couple living in my apartment building was selling the woman's slightly used bike. They had a big bag full of every accessory you could buy for a new bike. She obviously didn't know anything and walked into a bike shop with a credit card out and a SUCKER sign on her forehead. Nothing had ever been used or even opened from the packaging. They handed it all over with the bike for only a hundred and fifty dollars. Now I was in business.

Looking back on it, this new (to me) bike did have two problems. First, the pedals seemed kind of loose when I pushed on them. I wasn't too concerned about this because I knew the ride had different local bike shops working at multiple stops along the course to fix things that went wrong for the riders throughout the day. And second, and more importantly, the tires were massive mountain bike treads. This wasn't so obvious to me until I was at the event and every one of the other three thousand cyclists passed me with ease and commented, "Wow! Look at those tank treads. You probably should think about using a skinnier tire for a long ride like this."

"Thanks for the advice, Captain Obvious." Is what I didn't say back because I was always out of breath from struggling with every push of the pedal to try and keep up with the pack.

The day finally came, and it was the hottest day of the year. My family drove me to the high school where the ride kicked off and I huddled up with my team. They discussed how they usually planned to ride together for the first ten miles or so and then the faster riders would pull away. Some were also going to do the additional, optional, twenty-five-mile loop to make it an even hundred-mile trip for the first day. I would wait and see how I felt once I got to that fork in the road. (Spoiler: I did not do the extra loop!)

The gun went off and all three thousand riders were off. It was then I realized the error in my choice of bikes. Everyone was cruising past me with ease. Kids, as young as twelve, were coasting past as I struggled. It seemed like if I stopped pedaling for a second, my bike came to an immediate and jarring stop. I was pushing with all my might while I experimented with my gears to see if anything would help, nothing did. This was going to be a long, grueling seventy-five-mile day.

They had food and water stations set up every ten miles or so. This is what I was desperately waiting for. I took my bike over to the bike shop tent to have them do a quick fix on whatever was wrong with my pedal mechanism, making it so hard for me to keep my bike moving.

My expectations for how these "volunteer" bike mechanics

worked were a far cry from how it actually went. I truly thought I would be able to walk up and immediately get a full diagnosis of everything wrong, then they would quickly fix all the issues for no charge, and I would be on my way. In reality, they were equipped to patch flat tires, oil chains, and other simple maintenance items that came up throughout a long day.

When I asked them what might be wrong, they could tell with a few turns of the pedal.

"Oh man. Your crank is wah wah wah, wah wah wah!"

I smiled awkwardly and nodded along. He sounded just like the teachers in a *Peanuts* cartoon. I had no idea what any of it meant and I certainly wouldn't remember it a week later when I got the bike into a repair shop. I did pick up the final point he made before leaving me to work on the next bike in the line, a tire with a slow leak from picking up a nail in the street.

"You're screwed. I wouldn't ride that thing to the end of the parking lot, let alone another hundred and forty miles!"

And I thanked him for his help and continued on my way. The rest of the day went like this: Every rider blew past me from one rest stop to the next. They stopped and enjoyed a long rest, some watermelon and Gatorade, and some pleasant conversation among new friends. I splashed some water on my face and kept going to make up for lost time since I was going half as fast as them with twice the effort. I'd get towards the front of the pack for a moment until everyone started riding again and we would start the ritual over again. As each person passed by, each and every time, they would comment, "Wow, those tires are huge. You should get a lighter bike!"

We had three choices for sleeping arrangements on Saturday night. You could sleep in the Sandusky high school gym where the course ended, you could sleep in a tent out in the field next door, or you could get a hotel room in the area.

The rest of my team got a hotel room every year. They soaked in a hot tub, drank all night, and had their wives drive them home the next morning.

They never did the ride back and were impressed that I planned to make the return journey on Sunday. I didn't have the funds for a room and I think all the hotels were booked even if I did. I wasn't going to sleep on the gymnasium floor with hundreds of sweaty dudes. So I opted for the camping option.

One nice thing they offered was that you could throw your tent and a bag of spare clothes in the back of a big truck and it would be waiting for you when you arrived at the end of the first day's ride.

I didn't have a quality tent at the time but it was really warm so I wouldn't need much. My wife packed me with the tent that my daughters played in, out in their grandma's backyard. I didn't find out until that night when I was setting it up, they lost all of the stakes a few campouts ago. I got it all set up but the school is close to the lake, it was warm but very windy. I found a small tree in the otherwise barren field and broke a few tiny branches off of it hoping to MacGyver myself some usable stakes to hold the corners of the tent down.

They didn't hold and the tent rolled over many times throughout the long night. My weight was the only thing that held it in place. It was more like sleeping inside a giant beach ball than a tent.

The next morning, I woke up and felt awful. I didn't sleep well, I was sore, and my bike was still broken. I had to face facts. It was time to throw in the towel. I called my wife and asked her to come pick me up. I was an hour's drive from home and she had to get the kids ready so it would be a while. I told her it was fine. They were handing out breakfast and the school was buzzing with activity as the riders and volunteers were getting ready for their second day of riding.

I was amazed at how efficient everyone was this morning, however. It seemed like only twenty minutes had passed and all the riders had finished breakfast, packed up their belongings, and rolled out. The workers tore down the event tents and drove to set everything up at the finish line back at yesterday's start.

The town was quickly deserted and I was left to wait for my family to pick me up.

I found a metal bench that wasn't too uncomfortable and laid down with my feet hanging off the end. I had my broken bicycle, a small duffle bag of dirty clothes, and half the pieces of a little girl's play tent. I don't think I've ever felt as homeless as I did that morning.

My family showed up ninety minutes later and found me sound asleep on that bench. I was exhausted and relieved to see them. They were proud of me and I was proud of myself. It was a great event for a good cause and I was glad I did it.

I went back again the following year and was much more prepared. My goal for the second ride was to ride back the second day for the complete experience. And I did it. It was much more gratifying to ride through the finish line with a cheering crowd to greet us.

Nine of Diamonds

I grew up on eighties horror movies and inappropriate comedies. In those days, I had to walk three miles and hope the clerk had no qualms about renting R-rated movies to little kids.

My first two kids were both girls. They were alright but my wife got to them before I could and started them on *Baby Einstein* and *Blue's Clues* instead of *Creepshow* and *Tales from the Crypt*.

Five years later, my son was born and although he started with Disney Channel originals, when he was about five years old I started showing him some of my favorite movies.

We started with monster movies. He liked *Jaws*, *Godzilla*, and *Cloverfield*. We went to the theater on opening night for the sequel, *10 Cloverfield Lane*. He was ten years old and we expected more monster destruction. That's not quite what we got and John Goodman scared the living hell out of both of us.

"Where are the monsters!?" We asked each other. I think everyone in that theater was asking themselves the same question.

There were other movies that Nate enjoyed but probably

watched when he was still a few years too young. He stayed over at my parents' house for a weekend and came home singing "Jump in The Line" and "Day-O (The Banana Boat Song)." Jeanette looked right at me, "Beetlejuice, really!?" Thanks, dad.

We watched *Die Hard* with the family a few days before Christmas. My daughters knew better than to tell their Grandma about it but they got to her house for Christmas Eve a few hours before I got out of work and I showed up to a house full of nasty looks as he ran around the house screaming "Yippee-ki-yay! Yippee-ki-yay!"

For a short time, I tried showing him some things that were a little scarier. Jeff Goldblum's *The Fly* and *Signs* were two early attempts. Shortly after that, he complained to his mom that he couldn't sleep because he was having nightmares. She shut our late-night scary movies down right then and there.

When Human Centipede 2 came out on DVD, I was so excited to see it. No one had it available for rent and this was before digital movies were as prominent as they are today. I asked around at local libraries and they were shocked and disgusted that I would be requesting such trash. I tried to explain the plot of the first movie in case they didn't know but that just made things worse.

My friend, Justin, found it online somewhere and copied it onto a DVD for me. With extra room on the disc, he added the Hugo movie that just came out as well as a bunch of episodes of *American Dad*.

Jeanette was working retail at the time and was closing on the night he gave me the disc. I was going to let the kids stay up late to watch *Hugo*, but only if they were quick to eat dinner, take baths, and be a hundred percent ready for bed when mom got home.

I had all three of them lined up on the couch and had their full attention. I popped two bags of popcorn and poured them each a small cup of lemonade.

I inserted the burned DVD and searched the thumbnails to select the movie. The icons were generic movie reels with only a few letters of the titles underneath. *HU...* and the *GO* was cut off. I highlighted it with the remote and pressed play. I left the remote on the TV stand and squished onto the couch with the kids. The movie started an instant later.

I misread the label when I selected it. This HU didn't stand for *Hugo*, it stood for *Hu... man Centipede 2!* The movie didn't start with a title screen or any credits to warn me what I was about to show my children and their virgin eyes.

It starts with a guy watching the first movie and being motivated to try it himself. So the first scene is the climax of the original movie. The kids were horrified, desperately trying to cover their eyes and their ears at the same time. I lunged across the room using my body as a human shield to block their view as I fumbled with the buttons trying to stop it before we got any further.

I cut my losses. The kids finished their snacks and drinks while we watched one of their TV shows on video and I tucked them into bed.

I thought we stopped it before they saw too much, but the next morning as their mom was making breakfast and getting them ready for school, they had all sorts of questions, mostly about the digestive system.

Ten of Diamonds

For five years in the early nineties, I spent almost every summer night at my local dollar theater. These theaters are kind of a forgotten pastime now, but they would get movies a few months after their initial release. Tickets were only a dollar and the theater made all their profits on selling concessions.

The summer after eighth grade I spent all of my time in Fairview Park with my friend, Eric. We would hit our comic shop, Murray's, and then see whatever happened to be playing. I think we saw Aladdin fourteen times. I also remember seeing other favorites for the first time there as well; Edward Scissorhands, Forrest Gump, Indian Summer, and countless others.

As they say, all good things must come to an end. The theater was in a plaza that was being demolished to make way for a grocery store and where the single-screen theater stood was going to be the parking lot.

I guess there wasn't much publicity around its final days because no one seemed to know. But I knew and I brought a bunch of friends for the final showing.

My mom wrote for the local newspaper, *The West Life*. Having a news reporter mom had its pros and cons. When I was in elementary school she ran the newspaper club. That was pretty neat. And in middle school we had a surprise guest visit our English class, it was my mom and all the kids were impressed.

But, on the other hand, she also wrote editorials about her family life. One of these stories was about how her son called 1-900 numbers from our phone in the basement. These numbers were advertised on the back pages of magazines. Men would call to talk with a beautiful (?), seductive woman and have phone sex if they stayed on the line long enough. The charges were generally $3.95 the first minute and .95 each additional minute, but some of these numbers were connected to operators overseas. These carried the usual fees, as well as very expensive long-distance charges. The phone bill was outrageous because her son would sneak downstairs and call these women and talk for hours at a time. She didn't want to announce the perpetrator's name to the world so she omitted that it was my six-year-old brother. That was great for him but didn't go too well for me. I was ten at the time and all of my friends' parents who read the paper assumed I was the pervert that cost my mom hundreds of dollars.

My mom had found out about the theater closing and told me the night that was to be their last. The final movie to ever play at that theater was *Bad Boys*, an amazing buddy cop movie from 1995 starring Will Smith, Martin Lawrence (Fun fact: It was originally going to be Dana Carvey and Jon Lovitz. Could you imagine how different that movie would have been!?) and, the stunning, Tea Leoni.

My friends and I showed up expecting a packed house

with everyone in town sharing their favorite memories at the theater and saying their goodbyes. We found we were the only ones there and the staff was surprised and upset that we even knew they were going to close.

We talked them into giving us all free large popcorns since it was all going to be bulldozed within a week anyway. Between the popcorn, the candy we bought, and the Subway sandwiches we snuck in with us, there was a feast for each of us that evening. We were getting pretty rambunctious as the movie went on and most of that food ended up being dumped all over the floor.

As the movie was wrapping up, our friend, Ryan, got up to go to the bathroom. Fifteen minutes passed and he hadn't returned to his seat. During the final minutes of the movie, we heard a loud bang at the back of the theater. He brought a small screwdriver and unscrewed the seats from the floor. He was only planning on taking one but they were all connected and he had to take the entire back row.

If you've ever seen kids opening the emergency fire exit to sneak their friends into a dark theater, this was the opposite. We were using an entire row of movie theater seats, with armrests attached, as a battering ram to smash through the double doors and out into the rear alley. Mission Accomplished and high-fives all around! Then we remembered, we had to walk two and a half miles home, in the snow, with hundreds of pounds worth of dirty seats to carry the entire way.

We teamed up and got them to Ryan's house and down into his basement. I'm sure his mom was delighted. I haven't seen Ryan in years and don't know if his family still lives in the same house from 25 years ago but I like to think that those sticky chairs are still down there and they built a home theater around them.

Jack of Diamonds

In elementary school, I went to a speech therapist twice a week after lunch. I had trouble pronouncing my Rs and Ls. This was during recess on those days and kids would always ask where I was. For the first few weeks, I would tell them how I'd won a contest or got such good grades that I was in a special "Lunch Bunch" club and we got McDonald's and got to eat with some of the teachers and a group of high achieving students.

This only worked for a month or so, since no one else had ever heard of the club, including my friends that were much better students than me.

During these sessions and for homework, I had to write and repeat verbally a collection of words with the L and R sounds (Horse, Horse, Horse... Girl, Girl, Girl... and so on.) I had to really concentrate on pronouncing those sounds correctly and rolling my tongue on the problem syllables. On the last day of fifth grade, after two years of this, the teacher said that I had made enough progress to decide whether I wanted to continue with these classes in sixth grade or if I was confident enough to stop going. Without discussing it with my parents and with no hesitation, I exclaimed that I did not want to continue with these embarrassing classes in middle school.

The following year, on the very first day at my middle school, Homeroom was our first class of the day and had gone by without incident.

Second period was Social Studies. The teacher handed out our textbooks and we went over class rules and expectations, the typical first day of class type stuff.

These formalities were followed by the class taking turns reading one paragraph at a time, out loud, from the first chapter of the book. My greatest fear had come true less than an hour into my middle school career. As the kids took their turns before me and the order snaked down each aisle of desks, I counted out the students compared to the paragraphs and calculated which section I would soon be tasked with reading out loud to the entire class. I skimmed my few sentences, carefully, for potential problem words that I knew I would have to focus all of my prior pronunciation lessons on. There it was, near the end of my paragraph, one single word that, if said incorrectly, would determine my reputation and popularity and success going forward into the new year at my new school...

EARTH!

Everything became a blur. The other kids' spoken words were no longer heard individually. They flowed together and buzzed through my head as background noise. I could hear each student speaking, but really only noticed when they would stop and the next would start, getting closer and slightly louder each time. I was going over the word in my head over and over. Wording it silently to myself, practicing what I had learned, and rolling my tongue with the sound. Watching the clock all the while, praying that the bell would ring and save me from this torment.

My time had come. The kid behind me (one of the Therese twins probably, based on our last names. It was always Steve or Donna behind me.) finished and I waited just a moment, willing the bell to life, hoping that I would be saved by it. No luck. It really was time.

I started reading without having to think about the words, I practically knew them by heart by now. Just eyeing that "Earth" and getting my tongue ready to roll...

"URRRLLTH!" It was out there. Hanging over the class. I don't know if I spelled it correctly here, you have to imagine the word being spoken so incorrectly that it is unrecognizable to the human ear. Maybe try it the next time your mouth is numbed with Novocain at the dentist, or if you find yourself with your tongue ripped out of your mouth by Vinnie Jones in *Midnight Meat Train*, that is essentially how it sounded. The entire class was horrified at the sound and the teacher had to settle everyone down. Of course, that is when the bell began to ring, just a moment too late to do me any good.

The next period, before class had started. The three most popular girls in our grade came to me and the leader of the group sat, seductively, on my desk. Leaning in close, in a slight whisper, she explained that she was looking for someone to be her new boyfriend. She only had one demand, for her new beau to prove his love and dedication to her. "Just say one word, loud enough for everyone to hear. Just say UR-RRLLTH!!!"

I would remain single for the next four years.

Queen of Diamonds

When I was a senior in high school, I was shopping at my local comic shop. The store wasn't doing as much business as it had been. I didn't know it until many years later but this was in 1996 when the comic book crash was starting and the industry was going through a severe nosedive. There were so many comic stores that had popped up in the early nineties and the majority of them would be closed by the end of the decade.

I thought it was interesting that the owner had a Now Hiring sign in the window. I was looking for a part-time job with a good discount so I went into the store to inquire about it. He wasn't hiring for his store. He had a new business partner and they were selling home security systems.

That Saturday afternoon, a bunch of potential salespeople were invited to a free lunch at Denny's. I was, and still am, a sucker for a free meal so I was sure to be the first one there. I showed up with an open mind and an empty stomach.

The salespeople were very persuasive and I was eating up both my chicken sandwich and their pitch. They were only interested in the most motivated salespeople. People who were ready and willing to take a service that practically sold itself and turn it into a long-term career with a six-figure salary. The security systems were of great value. After all, how can you put a price on your family's peace of mind?

All we had to do to get involved was purchase the initial security demo. It came in a giant black suitcase and was a steal at only seven hundred dollars. I would travel to my customers' houses, people that would reach out to me and request an in-home demonstration, or, on occasion, I would set up these appointments with family members and friends. We would all be working solely on commission. We could make a certain percentage of every system we sold but they explained how we could make even more money by recruiting people to purchase the demo and start working directly beneath us.

The presentation went on for about two hours but I was convinced that this was my future within the first twenty minutes. I was ready to sign up and get started on my new career. I was only seventeen but I knew so many people that needed a quality security system. I also had friends that were both motivated and enthusiastic salesmen that would be perfect for this position. I was counting the earnings in my head even before I finished my plate of fries. There was one small problem, that modest introductory fee of seven hundred bucks.

I didn't have that kind of money but I was sure my parents would jump at the chance to invest in my future. My friend gave me the packet explaining everything we had discussed that afternoon and I hopped on my bicycle to ride home and start making my first cold calls.

I ran into the kitchen and told my mom all about the program I was about to get involved with. "You didn't sign anything did you!?" She asked in a panic.

"Not yet, I just need you to write out the check and I'll head back up to the store now."

"Jesus, haven't we taught you anything? This is clearly a pyramid scheme."

"No mom, maybe I didn't explain it correctly. I will sign up and both me and my friend get paid. Then I get my friends to sign up and all of us make a small fortune."

As I explained this, she pulled out a pen and started drawing stick figures on the back of the packet that represented my comic shop owner friend on top, me and the other new recruits under him, and my recruits, underneath. She then drew a triangle around all of us. It did look surprisingly like a pyramid but I wasn't going to be deterred that easily. Exhausted by my naivety, my mom started on the first page of the pamphlet and started highlighting every sentence that pointed to this being a scam. There was a lot of bright yellow marker all over every page.

I was crestfallen, she was right about it being a terrible idea. I had to call my contact and tell him I was sorry and couldn't get him the sign-up money. He was noticeably disappointed and asked me to return his paperwork, it was costly to print and he was going to pass it along to the next possible salesman he had lined up.

"Um," I flipped through the bright fluorescent yellow pages with SCAM! printed multiple times throughout each page. "I don't think you're going to want to reuse this one."

King of Diamonds

Every time I hear Stevie Nicks, especially her duet with Tom Petty, *Stop Draggin' My Heart Around*, I am thrust back in time to Saturday mornings in the early eighties.

I always watched my morning cartoons on our nineteen-inch, black and white, tube TV with rabbit ears down in the basement. It was an open area and instead of having walls to separate the different rooms, we had bookshelves with my mom's hundreds of books. These came in handy whenever we had book reports to do or needed something good to read. These "walls" were definitely not soundproof, though.

My dad lifted weights every Saturday morning while I was growing up and would play his records with the volume all the way up. This already drowned out any of the sound coming out of my television's tiny speakers but for some reason, he, with his superhuman hearing, noticed if I turned my volume up at all in the next room over. I was only allowed to watch if I sat in silence and enjoyed the A-side of *Bella Donna* on repeat as the unofficial soundtrack to all my favorite cartoons.

You know those catchy theme songs that are still stuck in your head after forty years. Well, I think of *Heathcliff* and

Leather and Lace runs through my mind. Smurfs came on during the third go-around of *Edge of Seventeen*. I often gave up trying to read the characters' lips after a few hours. He had stacks of Fantastic Four comics, from a garage sale, that I'd browse through and solve the Chips Ahoy maze that was the same on the back of each issue. I might not have been able to watch my shows with sound but I could breeze my way around those chocolate chips with my eyes closed.

At school on Monday, all the kids would be talking about the newest episodes from two days prior. I'd be eavesdropping, desperately trying to catch up on the details of what happened in each of my shows. I saw what was happening but couldn't pick up on the storyline. What I learned usually never matched the story that I created in my imagination. Honestly, I think the plots I made up were better anyway.

Ace of Spades

Anyone who has worked in retail knows that you can't really take sick days. At GameStop, we only had three members of management and we all worked forty hours a week. This meant that if one of us ever called off, there was no one to cover our shift without going into overtime, which was strictly forbidden.

I had just started working at GameStop again after my GameCrazy store closed. GameCrazy was owned by Hollywood Video and when all the video stores started closing, we had to close as well by default.

The previous manager at my store was known for calling off a lot and, being brand new to my staff, I didn't want to give the impression that I would ever fake being sick to get a day off.

When I lost my job at GameCrazy, my dad gave me his old car so that I would be able to get around to interviews and wherever I had to drive for my next job.

For years, my dad bought new cars. But, because he always wanted to buy new, he would pass on all the "bells and whistles". He would look at an itemized price list for each of the features on the car he was interested in and pick it apart line by line.

"Seventy-five dollars for floor mats? No thank you."

"Automatic windows? You think my arms are broken?"

"Automatic transmission? My grandpa told him that if you weren't doing anything with your right hand anyway, you could certainly use it to put your car in gear." I don't know that my grandfather had ever tried to eat a double whopper with extra mayonnaise while shifting into fifth on the highway.

"Cup holders? We won't be needing those." This was a little Kia with absolutely no frills.

Luckily, my brother worked at a shoe store at the time and got my dad great deals on shoes. He would buy multiple pairs of the same shoe if they were a good enough bargain and since we wore the same size, he would pass extras down to me occasionally. He gave me a pair that I wasn't necessarily impressed with, but I took them anxiously. The left one went straight into the trunk and the right, size ten, Adidas sat in my passenger seat. My cup holder problem was solved.

I don't know if it was something I ate, but one summer day I felt absolutely terrible. I was working a closing shift that day and had to be there at one. Despite my wife advising against it, I had to tough it out and go into work. If nothing else, I had to show the opener that I wasn't faking and trying to stick him with a twelve-hour, open to close, shift with no lunch break.

I drove five miles to Westgate Plaza where my store was. It was really hot out and I was leaning my forehead against the window as I went. I pulled into the parking lot in front of my store. It was at that moment that I suddenly had to puke. I wasn't able to get out of the car, open the door, or even roll the window down with the hand crank. It was coming and coming fast! In a sickly weak panic, I grabbed for the only thing within reach.

It was that size ten cup holder from the empty seat next to me. And I filled that shoe up to the brim!

My nose was running and my eyes were watering, but I must have vomited everything that had been stewing in my stomach all morning. That was a relief because my shoe was full and another drop would have overflowed up and over the sides.

The store was down the block from Magnificat High-school, an all-girl school that let the students walk to local restaurants for lunch. As I was slowly and carefully clambering out of my car with my shoe full of vomit, a large group of teenage girls walked by right in front of me. One of them looked over and soon got the attention of the entire group. They were shocked and disgusted at the scene unfolding in front of their eyes and they nervously picked up their pace.

I stumbled to the sidewalk and dumped my soiled shoe into the public garbage can. Thinking about my situation for a moment, I threw the shoe in as well. I knew I would never be able to clean it out and besides I had a backup left shoe in the trunk to take its place.

I entered the store, passed through the sales floor, and straight to the backroom to get cleaned up. My Third Key, Jonathan, saw me and immediately knew I was deathly ill.

"What are you doing here? You look terrible!"

"No, I'm fine. I promise I'm not faking."

"Yeah, no one is going to accuse you of faking anything. Go home!"

"Just give me a minute in the bathroom. I'll be right back up." I croaked as I went into the bathroom.

I was cleaning myself up and gaining my composure. Just as I thought I was going to be alright, the nausea returned. I don't know where it came from. I thought the tank must have been empty from when I was in the car just a few minutes ago. At least I was in the bathroom this time and had a toilet available.

Jonathan heard me through the door and yelled at me to go home. He would figure out coverage for my shift.

I made my way back home and slept the rest of the day. That might have been the only sick day I ever used over my twenty-plus years in retail.

I was feeling much better the next morning and returned to work for my opening shift. We had these large metal security doors that had to be rolled up into the ceiling, similar to garage doors. As I was pushing the heavy door up, I looked out the front window and locked eyes with the maintenance guy for the property who drove a golf cart around to empty all the garbage cans each morning.

The timing was perfect for me to catch him pulling the large clear trash bag filled with puke and a single shoe that was still oozing. He looked disgustedly at the contents of the bag and then looked at me. He couldn't have known that was my shoe, but my crestfallen face probably gave it away. I mouthed the words, "I'm sorry." silently through the glass to him.

Two of Spades

My son, Nate, and I have bonded over different video games most of his life. In recent years it's been *Resident Evil 4*. I got him to try it and expected it to be somewhat difficult for him. I knew this game well and looked forward to him getting stuck and coming to me for tips at certain parts. I would check up on his progress and was prepared for him to ask me for help when he was frustrated just like I was during my first playthrough. Needless to say, that never happened. He hurried through each new area of the game and even showed me secrets I had never seen during my many playthroughs.

He's better at games than Jimmy Woods in *The Wizard*. That classic Nintendo commercial starring Fred Savage and Christian Slater is one of my favorite movies and we've seen it many times. "We love the glove, it's so bad!"

Before *RE4*, when he was much younger, five or six, we played *New Super Mario* for the Wii. That game is perfect for little boys and their dads because it is multiplayer. I was able to drag him through the hard levels at the beginning of the game. Then as he got better and learned all the buttons, he started doing the heavy lifting and dragging me along. Damn those ice levels!

We beat the hell out of that game. We got all the special coins and finished the game 100%. The next day he opened the menu, selected our save file, and deleted all of our hard-earned progress. I was devastated! All that time and frustration and hard work went down the drain with a single mistaken push of the A button.

I could have screamed in utter horror but I bottled up my disappointment. I didn't want him to see my dismay. I thought he was going to start to cry when he realized the mistake he made. He looked back at me from where he sat right up close to the TV...

And he had the biggest smile on his face.

"I guess we have to beat it all over again. Right, dad?" He taught me that sometimes the journey is more important than the destination.

Soon after that day, he woke me up at dawn on a morning I had off work.

"Dad! We have to play Mario!"

"Okay, buddy. Just let me wake up and get dressed. You can get the game started."

"No, not the Wii game. The real-life game!" I wasn't sure what that meant but I got ready for the day and found he already had his shoes on. He was determined to get an early start.

He directed me to the nature center in the Metroparks and the "game" began. I was Mario and he was Yellow Toad. (He was always Yellow Toad and that was the theme at his birthday party that year.)

Rocks turned into Goombas, puddles were pits of lava,

and low-hanging branches were question blocks providing us with mushrooms and fire flowers.

Nothing was as it seemed. We were jumping off rocks and dodging imaginary fireballs. We took on bosses and were well on our way to saving Peach. We must have gone three miles and had been out there for over two hours. I was getting tired and hungry. I could only imagine he must have been exhausted on those little legs.

"Nate, look! Bowser's up ahead! It's the final boss!"

"No, dad. This is only the first level."

Three of Spades

I went to community college for a degree in education. I was torn between teaching young elementary students from Kindergarten through Fourth grade or middle school kids from Fifth through eighth. The problem arose that these two degrees, while they might sound similar, required very different courses. I took some of each and my credits were adding up towards my Associate's degree which was then going to lead to me transferring to a four-year college and finishing there.

I was in my mid-thirties and had been a retail manager for all of my adult life. I enjoyed working with the public and many of my best friends had started as either customers or employees. But I saw drastic changes starting to take place at the corporate office and at the district level. I didn't like the path my company was going down and I knew in my heart that it was time to start preparing for a "grown-up" career.

I really enjoyed three classes. First was a Math class for educators. The professor was also a middle school math teacher who talked about the struggles of teaching young teenagers. He taught us tricks to solve problems quickly and stay ahead of the smartest kids in the class. On the first day of class, he asked us who was actually taking his class because we desired to become a math teacher. I was the only one to raise my hand. Everyone else took the class because it was the easiest math credit.

The second was an online Ecology class. The professor in that class looked like he was only a teenager himself but he shared videos of his worldly adventures and made the subject fascinating.

The most interesting course, however, and the most useful, was an Intro to Education class. We spent most of our time in groups doing presentations. If we weren't comfortable talking in front of our peers, how would we ever hope to teach in front of thirty staring, judging, little kids?

We also had to find a teacher to shadow with for seven full school days over a two-month period. She had a list of contacts that we could reach out to and partner with a local teacher to complete this assignment. I didn't need help with this. I had been volunteering at my kids' elementary school for years and knew they would welcome me and appreciate my help.

I reached out to the principal and was directed to the administrative office of our school district. I was assured that they would find a teacher for me to work with, I just had to wait a few weeks for the proper paperwork to be processed. Everyone else in the class had started their volunteering duties and turned in their progress reports. I was still waiting for my assignment. Finally, I was running out of time and called the school to make sure things were in order. Something had slipped through the cracks and somehow the paperwork had gone missing. I didn't have a school to work at and all the professor's contacts had been claimed.

My brother's brother-in-law, Gary, was a math teacher on the other side of town. I called the school office and they accepted me in a heartbeat. I turned in my drug and background checks, ironed my nicest dress shirt, and arrived an hour early for my first day.

It was a third-grade class. I spent most of the class periods helping with the daily lessons. With about thirty students in each class, I couldn't believe it was possible to cater to so many different learning styles at once. I had a hard time just remembering anyone's name. I would hand out quizzes, collect homework, and spend time with a group of kids at the back of the room whenever they needed extra help with the previous week's lessons.

After a few classes, the children left for "specials," classes that varied by day: gym, art, and music. Then they had lunch and finally recess. The core teachers used this time to grade papers, eat lunch, and prepare for the afternoon classes. He didn't need my help for any of these things and I wasn't overly interested in helping. But I did want to spend more time with the students, enjoy an elementary cafeteria lunch, and play some dodgeball.

One week the kids were playing kickball in the gym. One of the boys looked to the gym teacher and asked what he would get if he kicked the ball into the basketball hoop hanging from the far wall.

"An automatic homerun." The teacher responded sarcastically.

With confidence, and on the first pitch, that is exactly

what he did. He kicked a hard, line drive across the large room, hit the backboard, and amazingly, it went in. All the kids went wild. I might have been the most impressed. It would have been awesome if it had happened by accident. But the way he called his shot like that, it was truly epic!

Lunch was my favorite part of my days at the school. The kids were excited to have an adult visitor sitting with them and we agreed that I would sit at a different table every week, so I could spend time with each group.

The highlight of these twenty-minute lunch periods was a game they all played called "firework". Everyone took turns saying a letter around the table. "F," "I," "R," "E," "W," "O," "R," "K!" Then, after the "K!" the next kid in order would explode with the loudest sound effect they could muster without causing a scene and attracting the attention of the lunch monitor. This went on until all but one of us exploded and there was one winner.

Firework was great fun and they had a few variations if we had extra time. "Bad Boys vs Good Girls Firework!" was a great alternative where we broke up into teams where even if you exploded early, there was still a chance if someone on your team could survive to the end.

One thing I learned was that third grade is a state testing year. Many weeks that I was there were spent preparing the kids for these tests, then taking the tests, then rewarding them for working so hard on the tests with a class party or movie.

Because of these tests, I volunteered to help out with other grades or classes since there wasn't much for me to do while they worked on their tests in silence. When the teacher sent out an email offering my services, responses would flood in, begging for an extra helping hand. I made lots of friends with the grateful teachers and gained a lot of great experience with kids of different ages.

Over the next few semesters, I ran into many of the classmates from that course and would ask them how their plan of becoming a teacher was progressing. Many of them exclaimed that after spending time in a real classroom setting, with real students, they lost any desire to become a teacher.

When this course started, we all thought it was too early in our education program to be shadowing in a classroom setting. Afterward, it made sense and saved many of those college kids a lot of money and time.

I had a great time helping out with those kids and learned a lot about myself and what teachers dealt with.

After getting my Associate's, it was time to transfer to a four-year college. I would have to start going to school full time, and my grants were running out. I lost the wind from my sails and knew it was time to find a new career that didn't involve retail or teaching.

After learning the game of Firework!, I was eager to teach my family and friends. My kids and their cousins played on the Fourth.

And the next time we were at my parents' house, I explained it to my mom. Everyone else in the room already knew how to play. While I explained the simple rules, she nodded along, confirming that she understood.

I started the game, "F."

Mom was next in the circle, she paused for a moment. And responded,

"F... You!"

Four of Spades

I've spent many afternoons helping out in my three children's classes over the years, mostly in first through fourth grades. I would go once a week to help with math, read to the kids, and eat lunch with them.

The highlight of the year for me was Halloween. I own two books that I would bring into school and read to the students.

The first one is called *World War Won* by Dav Pilkey. It was the first book he wrote when he was still in high school for a young author contest when he lived only a town over from where I grew up. He came to my school and read it to our third-grade class. This was long before he started the *Captain Underpants* series, but all the kids knew him and it made for a pretty neat story. Also, the book has a great message and cute pictures.

The second is *Halloween* by Jerry Seinfeld, a picture book based on his stand-up routine about his Superman costume, trick or treating, and eating way too much candy. One of my favorite memories of reading this book was when my oldest daughter was in third grade and I was introducing it to the class. I asked the children if they knew the Seinfeld TV show and they stared back at me without a clue. Then my daughter yelled. "He's the guy from The Bee Movie!" and they all went crazy.

The teachers always seemed to appreciate my time spent with the kids. It was explained to me that none of the other dads were ever able or willing to volunteer and so it was important to have a male helping out in the classroom. That, and they were able to use that time for other work or to take a much-needed and well-deserved break.

One year, I was there for my son's class and they were getting ready for the annual Halloween Parade. This is when all the kids change into their costumes and walk through the halls showing off to all the other grades.

New for that year were these skin-tight spandex onesies that were often green like an alien or superhero-themed. The point is, these costumes can't be worn over clothes as they really are skin tight. And I mean skin tight!

Somehow, I got voluntold to go into the boys' restroom and make sure they were behaving and staying on task. The boys were understandably skittish about changing in front of each other and waited for the single stall to become available. This was taking forever and time was running out. I didn't want them to miss out on the parade and was getting impatient with them.

I exclaimed in my most authoritative voice, "We don't have time to wait for the stall! You have to take your pants off now!"

This will not be the only time throughout this book that I yelled something inappropriate as someone walked into the room behind me. This time it would be the vice-principal of the school. I looked at him with an embarrassed and terrified look, trying to communicate with my eyes that I was not, despite the current situation implying otherwise, a pedophile left alone with a classroom full of half-naked second graders.

"No, you're right." He said to my relief. "Hurry up boys, strip down!"

Five of Spades

Sam Raimi's *Evil Dead* holds a dear place in my heart. I don't like it nearly as much as its sequel, but it has gotten me in hot water more than once and so I respect its persistence to keep causing me trouble forty years after its original release.

The first time I heard of the *Evil Dead* franchise was in the fourth grade. I used to walk three miles to York Video. York was further from my house than two other video stores, but worth the extra distance because they had the best horror section in town.

I actually found *Evil Dead 2: Dead by Dawn* before the first one. It was on the new release wall with a skull on the cover of the VHS tape. What really caught my eye was the short blurb in the lower corner:

"If you like *A Nightmare on Elm St.* You'll Love *Evil Dead 2!*" I felt like they were talking directly to me, a ten-year-old who had recently seen and was addicted to everything Freddy Krueger. I snatched that off the shelf and went to the general horror section for the original. With both movies in hand, I walked straight to my friend Mark's house, down the street from me, to show him the wonders that I had found. I knew I would only have time to watch one movie that night, so I lent him the first one (without the Elm Street comment on the box) and took number two home for myself. The next morning, we agreed, we would meet up and exchange the tapes.

I watched *Evil Dead 2* twice that night, maybe I did have time after all. The box was right, I was in love! This movie blew my mind. Both the gore and the comedy were spot on. Ash was my new hero and I would be repeating his one-liners for months afterward, to my mom's and teachers' delight.

The next morning, as promised, I raced down the street to Mark's. I couldn't wait to hear what he thought of the first movie and, more importantly, watch it for myself. I knocked on his front door excitedly, but no one answered. I heard muffled voices coming from inside the house and tried to catch what was being said. Suddenly, his mom opened the door, just a crack, about the width of a VHS tape.

"Please never come to our house again. And don't talk to Mark at school from now on." She said slowly and clearly so that I would understand. She then threw the tape through the small opening and hit me in the chest.

I took both videos home with me and put the first movie into the living room player. I soon realized the issue. The first *Evil Dead* is not nearly as light-hearted and funny as the second. While I was watching Ash fight his possessed hand and laugh along with the lamp, Mark and his parents got to enjoy a good old-fashioned tree rape scene.

My "lifetime ban" wouldn't last more than a few weeks, but I definitely didn't get to pick movies to watch at his house during sleepovers ever again. We were back to watching episodes of *Mr. Wizard* and *The Monkees.*

More recently, I went to a Horror Marathon at a one-screen theater in Columbus. They ran 24-hour marathons closer to Halloween, but in the Spring, they did smaller ones. A few years ago they did the *Evil Dead* trilogy. I took my friend Jim, a fellow hard-core horror fan, and my eleven-year-old son. We had watched Ash in *Evil Dead 2* a few years before and he loved it. I had forgotten how crazy the first one was. He was, by far, the youngest kid in the audience and was noticeably shaken by the gore.

The guy next to us leaned over to him and told him to close his eyes and wait two hours, the next two movies weren't going to be nearly as bad. I don't know if my son has ever been able to look at oatmeal the same way again.

Jim and I certainly had a great time. And, despite what he said at the time, my son loved hanging out with us until seven in the morning after six hours of Ash, classic horror trailers, and three hours in the car each way.

Six of Spades

I don't have many great fatherly moments that I'm overly proud of but this story is about one of those days.

Emily really liked to read. She must have gotten that from her Grandma Templeton. She started young with the *Magic Treehouse* series but when she got older, she moved onto the young adult novel series called *Miss Peregrine's Home for Peculiar Children* by Ransom Riggs. She loved these books so much that she started an online fan club website about them.

The author was going to speak and sign autographs at a bookstore in Cincinnati, about a six-hour drive from Cleveland. But it was on a school night and we had serious doubts about the logistics of a twelve-hour round trip.

I was able to get the day off from work and picked her up before lunch at school. We stopped at the gas station to fill up our tank and stocked up on snacks and Mountain Dew for the road. The drive wasn't bad. The only eventful moment was when we came up behind a log truck and I flipped out. She didn't understand why so I had her watch the highway scene in *Final Destination 2*. That made her feel good about the second half of the drive.

When I asked my district manager for the day off to go,

she recommended we visit Loveland Castle. It was a beautiful castle, complete with a dungeon in the basement, multiple floors, and a small gift shop. We had a nice afternoon exploring the building and the surrounding property.

She had spent some of the car ride researching fun places to eat dinner and we had a few in mind to choose from while we waited for the book signing event to start. We found the plaza where the store was located and wanted to find one of the restaurants nearby so we wouldn't be late coming back. She was getting nervous that we would miss Ransom speak to the crowd so we stayed within walking distance.

We ended up eating at the Boston Market next door. Which was just fine with me, I love their turkey and I LOVE their mashed potatoes. Just as long as it's all drowning in gravy so I guess it's fair to say I really just adore gravy.

After dinner we walked over and joined the crowd in the center of the enormous sales floor. Young teenagers were milling around shoulder-to-shoulder. They were excitedly discussing their favorite parts of the series. Someone had mentioned hearing about the event on a fan site and it was the site that my daughter had started. It was really neat seeing her interact with friends she had met online from many different surrounding states.

Ransom Riggs stood on the landing of a staircase that went up to the second floor and talked about his books and the movie that was going to come out in a few weeks. As an added bonus, his wife, Tahereh Mafi, was there and spoke too. She is also a young adult fiction writer and Emily was excited to buy her book and get it signed as well.

It was a really fun event and both authors took time with all their fans showing that they really cared.

After waiting in the long line and getting our promotional swag, signatures, and a picture with both authors, it was just past nine o'clock and we still had to drive home and get some sleep before school and work the next day. I pulled the van out of the parking lot and entered our home address into the GPS.

"Estimated arrival time: 3:30 a.m." the screen flashed.

"Don't worry dad, we're in this together. You can count on me to..." And she dozed off.

I drove off into the night. Speeding North-East up Highway 71. If you haven't read the *Miss Peregrine* series, it's about a school of children with unusual abilities. It takes place in 1940 and a bomb is dropped on the school. Peregrine is able to create a time loop so they relive the same day over and over again.

Emily woke for just a moment and looked up at me. "Dad, if I could relive any day for the rest of my life, it would be today. I love you." And she fell back asleep.

That drive home didn't seem so long after all.

Congratulations! You found the hidden bonus I promised in the story about my fight over the *Choose Your Own Adventure Book* (Q♠).

That must mean:

1. Your grit and determination led you on a tireless journey of exploration.   Or...
2. You cheated and are reading these stories straight through and stumbled upon it.   Or...
3. This book has become such a great seller that when you Google my name, it no longer says, "Who the hell is she!?" and now offers the location of this hidden gem.

This is the one that started it all. I wrote this back in 2017 when I told my first story to an audience. My friend, Laura, invited me to tell a story for Story Club Cleveland.

I think I did alright and as a "featured performer," I made about eighteen bucks that night. It wasn't enough to quit my day job, just enough to get me and my wife a pizza for dinner on the way home.

This is the script I used as my guide. Check out the video with the QR code at the end of this book (Red Joker) and you can see how it turned out.

I am very awkward when talking to adults, but I blame it on the weather. I just don't care about the weather and that is all people ever want to talk about. When a stranger makes small talk about what the weather looks like, I talk about one of two things, a fact from a Snapple bottle cap, or, if the person seems really smart or like they drink a lot of Snapple, the most interesting thing I know, which is that ducks have corkscrew-shaped penises. So if you have ever talked to me in an elevator or in line and thought I was pretty weird, it's probably your fault for being boring. I have been limited as to the damage I can do to my teenage daughters' reputations because my wife usually takes them out to girl scouts and other girly activities. But, when my son turned six, my wife started signing him up for more stuff that I was expected to take him out into public.

Cub Scouts has been the thing that he has really grown to love, which makes me a Cub Scout dad, whether I want to be or not. Except, we aren't called Parents, we are called Akelas. Now, there are two types of Akelas in scouts. The leaders are usually Military, Police, or Firefighters, they are Resourceful, Strong, Awesome knot-tiers, good role models for the boys to look up to. Then there is the group I clearly fall into, the dads who enjoy an hour of free babysitting every other Tuesday night.

But these Navy Seal Akelas are experts at manipulation as well as leading night hikes and doing owl calls. Which is how I got tricked into becoming a Cub Scout volunteer, regardless of my lack of any desire or ability. I took one hike with the Pack Leader and came out of the woods as the Master of Ceremonies for the Pinewood Derby. Running the Derby only takes one weekend a year... And of course, an online training course.

So, I imagined the online training to teach me how to build a cabin, cure poison ivy, and other manly outdoorsman things that the elite scouts seemed to know from birth. But logging into the website, I found a much different training experience. Basically, all the Cub Scouts of America cares about is that you "Don't Touch the Boys!" and you are never, under any circumstance to go off alone with a scout, because you would definitely touch him and they would definitely get sued!

I got it; my training is complete! After three hours of online training, I now know the foundation of Cub Scouts "Do Not touch the kids!"

Our second year of Scouts starts and my son and I are ready for our first Cub Scout camping trip. Cub Scout camping in Cleveland often takes place at Beaumont Campground, which according to an Eagle Scout friend, was land previously owned by the Army. But it was always too marshy for them to use, so they donated it, along with the ten million mosquitos, to the Scouts. Most families come out on Saturday morning, but my son and I take the opportunity to go out on Friday night because we know there won't be many kids there on the first night. To our pleasant surprise, there are only two first-year, six-year-old scouts and their intense outdoorsman fathers. We set up our tent without incident, eat our packed dinner, and I sit with my fellow Akelas while Nate goes off to play with his new friends.

These two men introduce themselves. One is a cop (not a policeman, a cop. He's not the guy who teaches safety town every summer.) This dude has been transferred right out of a movie to this campsite to make me look like a sissy and being slightly bigger than The Rock, it's working. The other guy isn't nearly as huge or intimidating, but he is on some sort of emergency utility crew. When sewer pipes explode in the middle of winter, he's the guy who goes out and fixes it. So he has done more physical labor in one shift than I have done in my entire life. Of course, this is when they ask what it is I do to keep our fair city safe and running smoothly... Um, I'm the manager of a video game store. Pretty much the opposite of what either of these guys do. They are clearly disappointed and think I'm a piece of crap. I was encouraging our nation's teens to stop doing homework while also driving up childhood obesity across the country. They don't have to say it, they give me the same look of disgust that moms and wives have been giving me for years. The kids are off running into the marshy woods and swinging sticks at each other. I yell to my son to stop and the guys tell me to "Let the boys be boys!"

The utility guy says: "Looks like we're going to have good weather tomorrow." To which I naturally reply, "Pretty neat how ducks have corkscrew penises." I get that look again, this is not going well, and the night is still young.

Around this time, it starts getting really dark which means two things come out at a camp in the middle of nowhere. Stars! Beautiful, bright stars! More than you could count in a lifetime. It was magnificent, this was why we came out here a night early. Just lean your head back and enjoy... when POW! The brightest flashlights, probably police issued, are blasted right into my eyes. My eyes had been adjusting to the darkness all night, and this had completely blinded me! "Hey guys, you don't need those lights. Just come sit by the fire and relax." I look to the other fathers to step in and yell at their kids... "Let the boys be boys." What the hell? Did they take a different training course than me?

The two guys have to move their cars and ask if I'm ok to

watch after their two young kids… "Absolutely not!" So they leave me alone with the three kids anyway, still running in and out of the woods. Now they are telling scary stories which involve a different monster each time knocking on the door and Pooping Everywhere! Then they ask me to tell a real scary story, shine the damn light in my eyes, and run back into the woods.

After fifteen minutes of this, I finally agree to tell them a story if they will sit down. All three of them sit down and are ready for a good scare, or are they?

I make up a story about the founder of the camp, Mr. Mont. But all the kids called him by his first name, Bo! He loved the kids and they loved him, but mostly they loved the ice cream he gave them at the end of a long hot day. He kept an ice cream scoop hanging from his belt at all times. But the one thing that Bo absolutely hated was being blinded by flashlights every night. And on the last night of his first summer running the camp, he lost it. He hid in the outhouse and when the kids went to the bathroom in the middle of the night, he chanted: "Lights in the eyes, lights in the eyes, when your dad wakes up, he'll be surprised!" and scooped them up in an old wet sleeping bag! He dragged them to the far side of the pond and scooped out their eyes with his ice cream scooper because if he couldn't enjoy the stars, they never would again. The children still live over in the rotten old cabin with Bo, blindly stumbling through the damp forest at night. But he still comes out to find more kids who insist on flashing their lights in the Akela's faces and waits for them to get out of the tent and walk to the outhouse at night.

This is when the dads return to their kids running in a circle screaming. "We're all gonna die!" "No one can go to the bathroom tonight!" "We have to go in your sleeping bag!" "I'm throwing my sleeping bag in the fire!"

The men were so pissed and said the kids were sleeping with me tonight. I corrected them, saying that if I was left alone with their kids, I might be inclined to touch them. Let me tell you, that sarcasm was not appreciated considering everything I had said up to that point of the evening.

Everyone went to sleep, the little kids both wet themselves that night and the dads told everyone who showed up in the morning about my terrible story.

Saturday went better, we hiked and played field games. All the parents avoided me. It was really fun.

Then everyone's favorite part of the entire weekend came. The boys do tell jokes around the fire. Most of the jokes are stolen from the back of the current Boy's Life magazine, which we all are required to subscribe to, so none of them are very creative. From the first joke on, my son is waving both arms like a madman, trying to get picked to tell his joke. I didn't even know he knew any jokes. Finally, the scout leader says that there is only time for one more joke. My son is about to explode when he finally gets called up. As he's working his way up to the patch of grass by the fire that serves as our stage, I am seeing my son's life play out in quick snap-shots, like in Run Lola Run. Nate telling his hilarious joke. Nate signing his contract for a starring role on his first TV show. Nate accepting his golden globe and thanking his Dad for taking him camping. He makes it up there and with confidence in his voice he asks: "How do you get the milk out of a cow?"

Everyone at once: "We don't know, how do you get the milk out of a cow!?"

"You kick it in its Milk Maker!"

Ooh, there was absolute silence. You could literally hear the crickets. Everyone slowly got up and left the fire and got in their cars or tents, just as angry as the night before, but tonight there were fifty people instead of just four. He seemed kind of oblivious that his joke was so awful. When we finally got into our tent and tucked into our sleeping bags, I asked him: "Where did you hear that joke, buddy?" "I don't know dad, my brain just told me."

And this is what my wife has had to deal with ever since from her son and her grown man-child husband always telling terrible jokes and stories.

Seven of Spades

The pinnacle of my life as a comedic genius was in a diner eating breakfast on a rock-climbing trip to West Virginia with my dad and his friends. I was nine years old.

I was just getting into horror movies, after watching *C.H.U.D.* with my dad. It's funny how I can't remember names to save my life, but I will know that *C.H.U.D.* stands for Cannibalistic Humanoid Underground Dwellers until the day I die.

We had rented *Creepshow 2* on video from the Dairy Mart by my house. For those not aware, *Creepshow* was a horror anthology movie written by Stephen King and directed by George Romero in 1982 and the sequel came out in May of '87 (I had to Google the release date.) I hadn't seen the first one at that age, but the box for number two had me and my dad intrigued. *Creepshow 2* has three stories and short animated scenes as a wraparound where Billy was being chased by bullies while the Creep shows up to introduce the next story.

The third story is called The Hitchhiker where this lady is driving home after a night with a male prostitute (This all went over my head when I was little.) and she runs over a hitchhiker in a yellow rain jacket, by accident, when she drops her cigarette in her lap. Of course, she drives away and tries to justify what she has done to herself. The hitchhiker pops up from the front of her car, saying, "Thanks for the ride, lady." Naturally, she flips out and runs him over again. He continues this for her entire ride home, getting more mangled and bloodied throughout the story. Each time he returns, he yells "Thanks for the ride, lady!" and it's more gargled each time as he takes more and more damage, along with her car. Finally, she gets into her garage and opens her car door, sure she imagined the whole thing and he is under the car and kills her, while gurgling blood and again screaming "Thanks for the ride!"

Where was I? Oh yeah, The Western Pancake House near New River Gorge, West Virginia.

So my dad and all his friends each ordered a stack of pancakes and the waitress brings them out with an ice cream scoop of butter on top of everyone's order. You can ask for no butter, but it never matters. All the years he has gone to this diner, they always put these huge scoops of butter on the pancakes! Knowing this, my dad will ask for an extra glass of water and drink it down quickly so that everyone at the table has somewhere to put all this excess butter. As the group is scooping their giant balls of butter into this overflowing cup, I say to the waitress...

"Thanks for the butter, lady! Hey lady, thanks for the butter!"

I think my dad was the only one at the table who had seen the movie and understood the reference. But he thought it was hilarious.

To this day, we still say, "Thanks for the (fill in the blank with whatever we get too much of that we didn't even want in the first place), Lady!"

Eight of Spades

I've always loved exploring garage sales all afternoon with my mom during the summers when I was young.

I delivered the weekly newspapers every Thursday when I was growing up, partially so my mom would have first dibs on the paper, TV guide, and most importantly the garage sale listings. I would be up at 4:00 in the morning to deliver two streets worth of papers, about sixty houses, while my mom would use different colored markers to circle the sales we would get to first and find the addresses in her battered and worn, red map book.

Then, after my work was done, we would head out, avoiding the "No Early Birds!" listings as most sales wouldn't start until 9:00 and we were starting at about 7:30.

My mom had always liked garage sales. My dad always said she could squeeze the piss out of a buffalo nickel! I didn't fully appreciate this weekly ritual until one day when I was in kindergarten. I was at recess to finish out the half-day of school after an afternoon of watching *Today's Special* and *Letter People* (This was the early '80s before kids were expected to learn long division in pre-school.) My mom pulled up on her bike (anytime I mention a bike, I mean a bicycle. My mom didn't drive until much later and I've never driven a motorcycle. Bikes, however, are sure to come up often throughout this book.) She had asked the teacher if I would be able to leave school early for a surprise that she had waiting for me at home. The teacher was okay with it and so we walked down the street to our house.

She had found Castle Grayskull along with most of the He-Man action figures and lugged it all home in the basket on her handlebars.

This would change my six-year-old life forever and I would enjoy many afternoons out with my mom for years afterward. Always looking for a similar holy grail of toys, but also just spending quality time with my mother that was worth much more than anything I could hope to find in those old garages.

It was 2010 and my kids were outgrowing their toys, I was outgrowing my DVD collection, and the family was outgrowing our apartment. It was time for us to hold a garage sale of our own.

I felt like Tim Owens must have felt when he replaced Rob Halford and joined his favorite band, Judas Priest, in '96. It was my time to put my years of garage saling experience to good use and show what I was capable of.

Living in an apartment, we didn't have a garage from which to peddle our wares. We packed up the minivan and made multiple loads of crap to my mother-in-law's house. This plan was going to help us accomplish a few different goals. We got to clean out our cluttered apartment, we were going to make some extra cash for that summer's fun with the kids, and we were hoping to convince Jeanette's mom to get rid of some stuff as well.

The front yard was cluttered with toys, outgrown clothes, books, and movies on both VHS and DVD. We went into Pam's house and gently suggested she offer some items of her own for sale.

After lots of persuasion, we talked her into parting with five items. She agreed to (1) an old tube television that was up in the attic It was broken, two hundred pounds, and had the super-sharp plastic on the bottom that practically cuts your fingers off whichever way you tried to carry it. (2) A cradle that I swear was straight out of a haunted orphanage that was designed to torture babies. The bars were perfectly placed at just the right width to trap a baby's head in between and it didn't rock anymore, but kind of jolted back and forth roughly. (3, 4, and 5) Three worn paperback romance novels.

The TV didn't even make it outside. I got it halfway down the stairs and she changed her mind and had me take it back up. After fighting with the cradle to get it out the front door, it sat in the driveway for ten minutes until someone asked if we would go down on the fifty-dollar price point. She immediately started wheeling it back towards the house, explaining that it was an antique and they paid double that price in the store. Back inside it went.

The sale was turning out to be a big success. I was having a great time and selling tons of stuff. Knowing that we weren't going to bring anything back home with us, I was selling it cheap. For toys and stuffed animals, I priced them based on size. Anything small was a dollar. But the bigger and bulkier it got, the cheaper it was.

"That Giant Gorilla we won at the carnival? Here's two bucks, get it out of here!"

The same went for my DVDs based on quality. "That movie is awesome, five bucks. Oh, this one is terrible, take a quarter and find the closest dumpster to drop it in."

All my books were a quarter each, but she wanted three dollars each for her romance novels. Which was funny because they were the worst books on the table. I had a few people show interest until I told them the prices and they dropped them like a hot potato. We only had a few hours left before closing time and a woman was looking over our extensive romance selection of books.

"How much are your books?"

"Just a quarter each. Oh, sorry. Except for those three, those are three bucks."

"Three dollars for these shitty torn books!?"

"Okay, I'll do all three for five bucks total."

"I'll give you a quarter each and you're lucky to even get that."

"Alright listen. Let's do all of them for a buck."

I did it, she agreed and paid. I pulled eight singles out of my pocket and folded them up with the single dollar she had given me. I hopped up to the front screen door and announced that I had sold the books and had the nine dollars for her.

"Oh, you sold them all for three dollars each?"

"Yep, just like you said."

"That's very interesting since I had the window open and was listening in on your conversation the whole time."

She was upset and I was caught red-handed. She snatched the full nine dollars out of my sweaty hand and sent me back outside to finish the day and take everything we hadn't sold to Goodwill.

But I didn't have to carry those damn books back up to the attic so it was well worth it.

Nine of Spades

Much to the chagrin of my mom, there was nothing that my friends and I loved more during the fall and winter months than playing backyard football at Little Clague Park on Sunday mornings.

It bothers me that all these years later I still feel the need to add "backyard" to that sentence. In elementary school, a teacher asked the class if anyone played football. I raised my hand along with some of the other boys. Immediately after class was over, the other boys came and taunted me because they were in some sort of rec league and played officially and they had never seen me there so they knew I was lying. "I play football, dick! I just don't play with you rich pansies!" is what I didn't say to them. And now, thirty-five years later, I am always sure to mention that I play backyard, unsanctioned, football.

We had a decent-sized group of friends that would meet every week to play. But on the odd week that not enough kids were available, we would head over to another park, Tri-City Park. There was a giant hill and we would play king of the mountain. We would just throw each other down the sledding hill and do some cheesy wrestling moves on each other.

This was innocent fun until the kids from that neighborhood would come out with their sleds and we'd get them involved and things would eventually get rougher than they should have. It always seemed like the kids we didn't know got hurt and limped home to their parents and that was our indication that it was time to head home before the police were called.

One of my best friends in High School, and still is, was Steve. We had known each other for a few years before my sophomore year, but mostly because we both had mutual friends.

We really got to know each other well when we were both running Cross Country in '94. We both ran the mile for indoor, winter track and were running pretty competitively in early '95. Races were on Saturday mornings and I had just run a personal record of 5:15. I don't know what time Steve got that morning, but he was behind me.

The day after my mile PR, it was bitterly cold and snowy. These were some of the best conditions for a game of backyard football. The morning started off like any other. Everyone showed up and we picked teams. We marked off the end zones as straight as we could in the deep snow. And the game was on.

A few hours into the game, we were all getting colder and tired. We would be finishing up after another score or so. The other team got a touchdown and kicked off. I caught the ball in the center of the end zone and started running it back. I don't remember where everyone else was on the field at that moment, but it was just me barreling down the field with Steve as the only defender in my way. I didn't swerve one way or the other. I ran straight for him. He claims to this day that I pointed at him while screaming, "I'm comin' for you!!!"

He didn't know what to do and I was picking up speed and momentum. He fell down on the ground and curled up in a ball at the last possible moment. It was too late for me to stop and so I had a decision to make, I could kick him full strength in the ribs, or I could jump over him. I've never hit a deer with my car but assume it's similar to deciding whether to swerve or not. I jumped, and I went flying. My friends said I cleared about ten feet.

When I landed, I landed hard, on my shoulder, on a sheet of solid ice.

I'd never felt pain like that in my life. I couldn't move and laid there with my face in the snow. Everyone knew something was wrong and came running over to me. I was shell-shocked but not fully out of it. I knew that Steve was at fault for the horrible pain I was in and I called him over. He got close and asked what he could do to help. I was on my chest with my legs sticking out behind me. I shook my right foot in the air behind me slightly and asked him to put his head right at that spot. He did and I tried with all my might to kick him square in the face.

Unfortunately, I missed and wasn't able to trick him into coming that close again.

The guys helped me up and walked me home to my parents. Every step was a chore but mostly it hurt to move my left arm.

They took me to the hospital and X-rays showed that I had broken my collarbone and it was a nasty break.

The doctors put it in a sling and told me not to move it.

Collarbones heal on their own over a month or so. I was in better spirits once I got some pain medication in me and got into bed. I was disappointed though that I had just run such a fast race the day before and now I was out for the season, and who knew how long I would take to get my speed and strength back to where I was.

Steve did feel really bad about what happened and even brought me over a cake to cheer me up. It was a green sheet cake with little plastic football players on it, one of them upside down with his face and shoulder smooshed into the frosting.

That was a really creative cake.

P.S. After that failed kick to the face, I never did blame Steve for that accident. We were dumb teenagers and we were playing tackle football on a sheet of solid ice. One of us was bound to get hurt that day.

Ten of Spades

I always loved playing tag when I was young. All types really, but my favorite was Jailbreak. One day we didn't have a group of kids to play with. So my best friend, Mike, and I rode our bikes to Big Clague Park a few miles away and started playing one on one tag on the playground.

Whichever one of us was "It" would chase the other around the fenced-in area. We would run up the slides, climb up and jump from the very top of the jungle gym, and even use the other kids as shields to keep from getting tagged.

The thing I learned about tag at an early age was that the games were only fun if everyone involved was fully committed and competitive. This would get more difficult as I got older and my friends in the neighborhood started paying more attention to video games, cars, and dating than a good old game of hide and seek at Fox Hills woods down the street from where we grew up.

I remember my disappointment vividly when I was hiding from a group of friends in the woods at one of our local parks. I had found a pretty discreet spot to start the game while they counted to get us started. Soon, I heard them shouting that they saw me and that they were going to move in and surround me.

I was ready to start running away from them and was quickly thinking about my getaway strategy. As I looked around to get my bearings, however, it was clear that they were not as close as they thought because I certainly would have seen them approaching. I cautiously moved from my hiding spot and made my way back towards the entrance of the forest where the group of seekers had been counting.

Those bastards were still lounging around the picnic table, yelling on occasion to give the impression that they were actively on the hunt for me. I came out from my cover and asked what the hell was going on. One of the kids explained that he couldn't chase me through the woods because his silk shirt was too nice and it would get sweaty and might get torn if he caught it on a branch.

I don't think I ever hung out with that kid again.

But that was much later, in middle school.

We were still in the fourth grade and not getting tagged was still our top priority over going to the mall or spending time with stupid girls and impressing them with stupid silk shirts.

That day at the park we had tried to recruit other kids to play with us but no one was interested. More accurately, none of the moms wanted their kids running around the playground with a couple of roughians, who were there without any parents.

We played for a while without incident. Then Mike was it again and gave me to the count of ten before giving chase.

Any evasive strategies were well exhausted at this point and it became a test of speed and endurance.

I ran up the stairs to the platform about five feet up. I grabbed the pole as if I was going to slide back down to the ground but at the last second, I swung out and around to land back on the platform. The idea was to trick him into jumping off after me and I'd be long gone by the time he realized my plan. In my head, it was a foolproof plan.

"See ya, wouldn't want to be ya!" I was going to yell as I ran the other way while he fell five feet to the ground, humiliated.

It would have worked perfectly too. Except that there was a pipe that seemed to be attached at random and with no purpose but to catch little kids in the face when they tried to pull off sweet maneuvers on the pole. If that was, in fact, their intention for putting it there, it had done its job.

That short pole hit me right in the mouth. More precisely, I guess I hit it since it was stationary and I was the one moving.

It shattered my top front tooth on impact and my mouth immediately filled with blood and small pieces of tooth. I was hurt bad but at that moment I was more worried about saving my tooth so that it could be reattached.

In tears, I called for Mike to help me and we dug through the mulch for anything that looked like small fragments of the tooth that could be glued back together and saved by a dentist.

With a pocket full of bloody pieces, some wood chips, and probably a few cigarette butts, we rode straight home for help.

My aunt Vicky was in town from Colorado She helped my

mom get me into the car and on our way to the dentist. My dad was there as well but he didn't offer much support other than asking what any MAD Magazine reading dad of the '80s would ask when their son lost a front tooth.

"What me worry!?"

My family thought he was being insensitive at the time, but now that I have my own kids and a lifelong love of Alfred E. Neuman, I'd be lying if I said I wouldn't have asked the same thing.

The dentist threw away my pocket full of bloody tooth pieces but appreciated the thought. He was able to create an imitation tooth and attach it to what was left of the base of my original. He warned my parents that it would last a year or two, at the most, and then we would have to consider a more permanent solution.

It's been over thirty-five years since that day and that fake tooth is holding strong.

Jack of Spades

I was twelve years old in 1991. There was no bigger fan of the *Nightmare on Elm Street* movies and Freddy Krueger than me.

I saw the first movie at a sleepover with my friend, Mike, and his parents. I remember we had walked to our local video store, One-Stop Video, and were browsing the horror section. Mike found the movie and the cover looked creepy so we asked if we could get it. We also told his dad that he wasn't allowed to try and scare us. He said we could get it but assured us that he wouldn't have to scare us. This one would do that just fine on its own.

He was absolutely right. That movie scared the living hell out of me. I'm sure I didn't sleep very well that night in a strange house and knowing that even my dreams were no longer a safe place to hide.

We caught up on the next few movies and then got the fourth and fifth as soon as they were released on video.

Then, in September of 1991, the newest and last movie in the series had just been released in theaters. I absolutely had to see it on the big screen, And in 3-D!

The only problem was that my parents never took us to the

theater for movies and they certainly weren't going to start with a Freddy movie. I was on my own. I rode my bike to the closest theater that was showing it, AMC at Westgate. I asked for a ticket and my 3-D Freddy-Vision glasses and they audibly laughed in my face. You had to be seventeen or have a guardian to see an R-rated movie. At twelve I was never going to pass for seventeen and I didn't have an adult to watch it with me.

I left the box office. I walked out into the parking lot, dejected but not yet defeated. It was a busy Saturday afternoon and groups of people were walking from their cars into the theater. I approached a group and asked what movie they were going to see. Not Freddy and so I moved onto an older couple. I was hoping that anyone would take me under their wing and purchase my ticket to get me into the movie.

After a few failed attempts at recruiting an adult companion, the manager of the theater came out and confronted me for "harassing his customers." He was overly upset, screamed at me to leave, and expressed that I was now banned from the theater for life.

The next week in school, I was tormented by all the boys in my class talking about such an amazing movie. I don't know if "Spoilers" were a thing back in the early nineties but my asshole friends didn't seem to care. Freddy's origin. Robert England without his makeup. Carlos's ear. Alice Cooper! No detail was off-limits. I had to find a way into this movie.

The following Saturday I tried my luck at the other theater showing the movie. A Regal Theater at Great Northern Plaza. I tried the same plan I had the week before. I asked adults what they were seeing and if they would bring me in with them. I actually saw someone I knew from school with their mom and I thought I was in. She wasn't comfortable harboring a minor though, so I was back to square one.

Soon, two kids I knew from a couple grades above me walked up with Freddy Krueger t-shirts and plastic gloves. What were these guys up to?

They walked straight up to the counter and both asked for tickets for *Beauty and the Beast*. They looked back at me with a wry smile and winked knowingly. How in the hell did that work? They were wearing Freddy gloves for Christ's sake!

I was desperate so I tried the same tactic. "One for *Robin Hood*, please."

I got a ticket and hurried to look above all the theater doors to see where my movie was. Great Northern theater had a very long hallway that led to two smaller auditoriums in the back. These were reserved for older movies that were on their way out and movies that didn't need quite so many seats. Both of my movies were down this hallway. *Robin Hood: Prince of Thieves* and the modern horror masterpiece, *Freddy's Dead: The Final Nightmare* were directly across the hall from each other. There were only two issues: First, I was already banned from the other local theater for life because of this movie, I couldn't afford to get caught and banned from this one too, the only other theater within biking distance. And second, and more importantly, I didn't have the pair of 3-D glasses that should have come with my ticket.

I was so close and yet still so far away. I couldn't bring myself to enter the wrong theater. I walked into the Kevin Costner movie and sat down. I actually did like that movie a lot and probably remember it so well because of the circumstances surrounding it. It was one of the few movies I've ever seen by myself in the theater.

I did drink a large coke during the first half of the movie. I held it as long as I could but I was going to pee myself if I didn't run to the bathroom. I missed the final sword fight between Robin and the Sheriff. I went as fast as I could but returned mere seconds after the climax. I'd have to wait till it showed up at the dollar theater to find out how their fight ended.

The following week, I convinced my Aunt Jill to take me and my cousin, Manny, to see it. It was everything I knew it would be and I couldn't have asked for better movie-going companions. We all loved it, or at least she pretended to, for my sake. And I didn't dare order a drink during Freddy.

Queen of Spades

I haven't been in many fights and none as an adult. Tyler Durden would be disappointed. I do remember my first fight very vividly, however. It was in elementary school against one of my best friends at the time, Mark.

It started in the Maple School library, we were talking about the only thing eight-year-old boys talked about in the eighties, *Choose Your Own Adventure* books. One of these books, *Inside UFO 54-40*, mentions the paradise planet, Ultima. Somewhere, I had heard that none of the choices you made within the book would get you to this ending, but it was included and was the true happy ending. It was better than getting back to Earth to reunite with your parents and certainly better than getting cut in half by a trans-dimensional portal.

When I told my friend this, he disputed it passionately. The only logical way to resolve this spat would be an all-out fight after school!

We agreed to meet at the park down the street after school. And a few classes later, I had to check in with him for clarification over the most important detail when preparing for a brawl.

"Is this just the two of us? Or should we bring friends and family to fight at our side?"

"Um, Friends. I guess."

"Got it, I'll see you after school. You're dead meat!"

Now the race was on. I had to gather up all the kids I knew before he did. We lived on the same street and would be recruiting soldiers from the same pool of friends.

I got my buddy Mike and he had a few friends that would come with him. Then I hit the wall. Everyone I reached out to had already committed to fighting on Mark's side.

"Damnit!" The unofficial count was about forty for him to my four or five. Most importantly, and devastatingly, one of the members of his newly formed gang was Rob. I think that guy was shaving in the second grade and would tear through my group all by himself.

Our day at school ended and we took the bus home. We sat together like we always did. We took this opportunity to discuss our fight one last time before the main event.

"3:30?" Check.

"Little Clague Park?" Check.

"Wait, by the baseball field or the playground?"

"Playground. There are more places to strategize."

"Got it. Oh, are your people bringing weapons?"

"Um, I didn't even think of that. It didn't occur to me."

"We'll see what most of the kids have and decide then."

Everything was in order. But panic was starting to take over. I was in too deep to back out but I was getting nervous about the sheer amount of people he was bringing... And what kind of weapons was he thinking about!?

I got to the park as soon as I could and took cover down

by the creek that bordered the north side of the field. Keeping a close eye for my few friends to arrive. Mike came riding his bike down the long parking lot entrance and was the first on either side to show up. I scream-whispered for him to come over and take cover.

His buddy Alan was the second to arrive and I was starting to feel better about my chances. Neither of them had thought to bring weapons though, so one baseball bat (or one Rob) would even things out quickly.

It was probably only ten minutes, but the uncertainty made it feel like a lifetime. Then the tables took a huge turn in our favor. Two middle schoolers were riding through the woods on their bikes and we took the opportunity to ask them to join our party. They said they were always up for a good Outsiders-style fight and we were definitely happy for the older reinforcements.

The time had come for our epic battle to start and we were all getting antsy. We found Mark, my arch-nemesis since earlier that afternoon, on the other side of the playground. But where were his friends? Did he have his forty, weapon-clad, allies waiting in the woods for his war cry to attack?

No, they had not come.

He was alone and asked for more time to see if anyone would show up. I'm not sure where the expression "Better late than never." originated, but it might have been this afternoon at Little Clague Park. I could see that he was getting nervous and almost felt bad for him. Don't get me wrong, I was relieved and very grateful for my friends who would support me in a fight over something so stupid. But at the same time, I was empathetic and knew that I would have broken down in tears if our situations were reversed and no one showed up for me.

My posse and I were discussing strategy on who would hold his arms behind his back and who would get to punch him in the face first. This is when things started to escalate and slip out of my control.

The older boys were getting impatient and wanted to get the fight started. Mark pulled out his Boy Scout issued pocket knife, which had been used to whittle animals from bars of soap up until now. They flipped out on him for concealing a deadly weapon. He hopped on his bike and sped away to his house, four blocks away through our neighborhood.

The teenagers gave chase on their own bikes and saw him run into his house. I was still at the park at this time, but they went right up to the door and told his mom that he had started a fight and asked if he would come back to the park to face his enemy like a man?

His mom called my mom and she drove to the park and laid on the horn to get my attention. It appeared that the fight was over before it even really started. We drove directly to his house and we were forced to shake and make up.

Our moms asked what we were even fighting over and, at that moment, we couldn't even remember, which was probably just as well. Looking back on it, "He said there wasn't a paradise planet, Ultima, hidden in the pages of a book we were reading." probably wasn't a valid reason to get stabbed in the stomach.

This conversation ended with me running my finger across my neck toward him in front of our parents. At the time, I thought this meant, "Boy are we in trouble!" It didn't occur to me that this would be taken as a threat that I was going to slit his throat. It didn't go over very well and I think of that every time I see Drax's confusion in the Guardians of the Galaxy movie.

The next day, we returned back to the library and looked through the pages of the book. There it was, on page 101, Ultima! Maybe if we would have looked closer the day before, it would have saved us a lot of trouble.

Two important notes about this story:

We asked many of the kids why they never showed up and most said they thought we were joking or that they just didn't care.

However, some went to the wrong park. There are two parks on Clague Road. One was in our neighborhood, a big field with a few baseball diamonds, we referred to it as Little Clague. The other is much bigger with a pool, duck pond, and walking trails, Big Clague.

There was a big group of kids that wandered around that park looking for a fight that day, including Rob. (Thank goodness!)

And in honor of that *Choose Your Own Adventure Book*, and because this book will accommodate such a thing, there is a bonus story somewhere in this book that won't be found by picking a card from the deck. It is hidden to the best of my ability...

And if you don't believe me, I'll meet you at Little Clague after school.

King of Spades

A few years ago, I had major pain in a small area above my left knee. After months of tests, my doctor determined that it was nerve damage and prescribed me some very powerful pain medication. I had never taken anything like this before but the pain was unbearable and I was ready to try anything that might bring some relief.

I was warned that there might be side effects and that I had to wean onto the drugs slowly. I was supposed to report any extreme mood changes or suicidal thoughts.

I know people become hopelessly addicted to these drugs but I don't understand it. They didn't make me feel any better and just put me into a fog. The pain didn't go away, it just seemed like all my senses were dimmed.

Everyone who knew what I was going through assumed I had stopped working and was staying home. I've been working since I was a fetus and didn't know any other way. I kept going to work and was relying on two friends, Steve and Tyler, to drive me there and back.

I was using a walker because I couldn't put weight on my leg and even with that, I often couldn't make it down the long hallway to my apartment.

Once I got to work and sat at my desk, I generally got through the day alright. My team took turns checking up on me at my desk and would sometimes find me slightly slouched over, my eyes glazed, and a little bit of drool clinging to my chin. I was able to keep up with my work, but it wasn't pretty.

I often pushed my walker over to where my team sat and sat between two of their desks with my back facing the windows. During the evening hours in the summer, the sun would shine brightly through the large floor-to-ceiling windows. It would create very clean, defined shadows on the center of the floor.

With my head hanging low, and in my usual drugged stupor, I started making intricate shadow puppets with my hands and fingers.

This must have gone on longer than I thought and while in my head I was making amazing dinosaurs and an awesome silhouette of Abraham Lincoln, my coworkers were not so impressed with my temporary shadow art.

Another supervisor saw me making strange hand motions from across the office and came over to investigate.

"How are you doing over here?" She asked everyone in our general vicinity.

"Fine, we're all fine over here." The others answered nervously, exchanging glances with each other.

I wasn't all there, but I knew enough to see that she was concerned about me. She walked back across the office to her desk and I wheeled my walker behind her as fast as I could.

"Hey, how is it going?" I asked much louder than I should have.

"Fine. What's up?"

"Good. No, that's good. I'm fine too. We're all fine over there."

"Okay."

"Okay, yes ma'am! Everything is just fine!"

I knew I had to get off these meds and I called the doctor later that week. He told me I would have to wean back off it, similarly to how I had weaned onto it in the first place. I explained that I had run out of the pills earlier that week so I wouldn't be able to wean, but that nothing had happened when I stopped taking them. He seemed honestly surprised by that and offered some alternatives to what I had been taking.

I declined his advice and told him I'd go back to Tylenol. He wished me luck and that was that.

Acknowledgements

A special thank you to my daughter, Emily. She was a great help in reading and rereading these stories on the lookout for stray commas. She was also instrumental in formatting the pages for me.

Emily used her impressive editing, proofreading, and Microsoft Word skills to turn my gibberish into what you are holding now.

Thank you to Kenny Peris for drawing the amazing cover. It is exactly what I was hoping for. He does some great work. Check out his Instagram page: **@thekennethevan**

Thank you to my beautiful wife, Jeanette. She tolerated me while I tapped away on my laptop instead of paying attention to season three of Agents of S.H.I.E.L.D.

Thank you to Helena for filling me in on the Agents plot points that I missed each night.

Thank you to Steve Orlowski and Bridget Mullen for coming out to my first Story Time Cleveland talk. Your support that night meant more to me than you could have known.

Thank you to Emerson Emser. If you read one of these stories and thought, "He didn't seem too awkward that one time." Chances are pretty good that Emerson was by my side, providing a voice of reason and looking out for me.

I give Mathew Serback a lot of the credit for making this book possible. He started working with me at Heartland in April 2021 and we became instant friends. During one of our first talks, I learned that he is a published author with many stories available online and a novel.

He gave me a copy of his book in exchange for a Chinese lunch and it blew my mind. I then shared my two videos of me telling stories with him. He gave me very positive and supportive feedback which motivated me to continue sharing my stories.

Finally, thank you to my friends and family for unwillingly making appearances throughout this book. I appreciate you having a sense of humor in advance.

Calen Templeton

Red Joker

Cub Scout Camping
July 2017

Black Joker

Drive-In Movies

August 2017

About the Author

Calen and his Grandpa

When he was in Kindergarten, he traded his train conductor hat for his grandpa's fishing hat.